TABLE OF CONTENTS

NOW, OUR FEDERAL GOVERNMENT MUST BE BROUGHT BACK UNDER THE CONTROL OF THE PEOPLE.

Premise — from the U.S. Constitution

• "No person shall be held to answer for a <u>capital</u> or other <u>infamous crime</u>, unless on a <u>presentment or indictment</u> of a <u>grand Jury</u>..." — *U.S. Constitution, Amendment V.*

• "In all <u>criminal prosecutions</u>, the <u>accused</u> shall enjoy the right to a <u>speedy and public trial</u>, by an <u>impartial jury</u> of the State and district wherein the crime shall have been committed, which district shall have been previously ascertained by law, and to be informed of the <u>nature and cause</u> of the <u>accusation</u> to be confronted <u>with the witnesses</u> against him; to have compulsory process for obtaining <u>witnesses in his favor</u>, and to have the <u>assistance of counsel</u> for his defence." — *U.S. Constitution, Amendment VI.*

• "In suits at common law, where the value in controversy shall exceed twenty dollars, <u>the right of trial by jury shall be preserved</u>, and <u>no fact tried by a jury</u> shall be otherwise <u>re-examined</u> in any court of the United States, than <u>according to the rules of the common law</u>." — *U.S. Constitution, Amendment VII.*

• "<u>Excessive bail</u> shall not be required, nor <u>excessive fines</u> imposed, nor <u>cruel and unusual punishment</u> inflicted." — *U.S. Constitution, Amendment VIII.*

• "... and all <u>executive and judicial officers</u>, both of the United States and of the several States, <u>shall be bound</u> by <u>oath or affirmation</u>, to support <u>THIS Constitution</u>..." — *U.S. Constitution, Article 6, Clause 3.*

• "No <u>capitation</u>, or other <u>direct, tax</u> shall be laid unless in proportion to the <u>census or enumeration</u> herein before directed to be taken." — *U.S. Constitution, Article I, Section 9, Clause 4.*

Introduction

A trial jury is a jury impaneled to try an action or prosecution.

A grand jury reviews evidence submitted by the prosecutor and determines whether a person should be charged with a crime by an indictment.

There is no more valuable service a citizen can perform than to aid their community by serving as a grand juror or trial juror. The principle that a person has a <u>right to be judged by a jury of his peers</u> dates back to England in the Middle Ages and is guaranteed by our Federal and State Constitutions. By serving as a juror you are helping to preserve a fundamental right, to protect that right so it will be a safeguard for all persons, including yourself, should you someday find your property, liberty or life endangered.

Give your service as a juror the same attention that you would like from a juror if you were a party involved in the trial.

Serving on a jury is hard work. The hours are long and the pay is less than you would receive from an employer. There may be periods of waiting and you may become impatient. However, you should not allow such periods to overshadow the importance of your jury service.

The purpose of this booklet is to share what the author learned about the court system <u>and himself</u> as a result of his four month experience seated on the Grand Jury of the Cumberland County Superior County in Portland, Maine.

This booklet will answer a few questions you would likely ask when first summoned to report for jury duty.

What Kind of Court is the Superior Court?

In the United States there are state and federal court systems.

The Superior Court in which the author served is part of the Maine state court system.

The types of cases which can be heard in each court are specified by state and federal laws, which establish the jurisdiction or subject matter which each court system may handle.

Within the federal and state court systems, there are different types of courts, whose jurisdiction is also set by law.

The Superior Court is a trial court.

The Supreme Judicial Court is an appellate court.

The District Court is a limited jurisdiction trial court in which cases are heard by a judge without a jury.

What Types of Cases are heard in the Superior Court?

A criminal case involves an accusation that an individual or corporation has committed a crime. The party charged with the crime, called the defendant, is brought before the court by an information, a complaint, or an indictment.

The plaintiff in the case is the State of Maine represented by the grand jury, who in turn is represented by a prosecutor who may be either from the District Attorney's office or from the Attorney General's office.

A defendant in a criminal trial under our constitutional system is presumed to be innocent. The State has the burden of proving to a trial jury a defendant's guilt beyond a reasonable doubt.

The Summons

During the first week of December of 2013, I received a GRAND JURY SUMMONS from the MAINE SUPERIOR COURT/UNIFIED CRIMINAL DOCKET - COUNTY OF: Cumberland, Dated 12/2/2013, Number 54.

This GRAND JURY SUMMONS said that I was **"hereby notified that you have been drawn to serve as a Grand Juror in the Superior Court and/or United Criminal Docket"** and that **"You are required to appear on Monday, January 6, 2014 AT 8:30 AM at 205 Newbury Street, Portland, ME.**

This Summons was Stamped, *Sally Bourget, Clerk of Court.*

Continuing Text . . .

LENGTH OF SERVICE: The Grand Jury sits the 1st full week of the month for 4 consecutive months. The court day normally runs from 8:30 AM to 4:00 PM.

EXEMPTION: Under Maine Law, if you are 80 years of age or older and wish to be excused from jury service, notify the Clerk in writing immediately upon receipt of this summons and you will be automatically excused from jury service. If you do NOT wish to be excused, then you should appear at court as directed in this summons.

EXCUSES: Jury service is both a duty and privilege of citizenship. If you are requesting an excuse for medical reasons, you must submit a doctor's certificate. All other requests for excuse from jury duty must be submitted to the Clerk in writing immediately upon receipt of this summons. Excuses will be granted only by the Clerk prior to reporting for jury service. Excuses will not be granted by the presiding justice on the day you report for jury service.

EXCUSES MUST BE FILED WITH THE COURT BY:
Friday, December 27, 2013
Cumberland County Superior Court
PO Box 287
Portland, ME 04112-0287

According to Maine law, failure to appear or to complete jury service may constitute contempt of court and may be punished by a fine and/or imprisonment.

SEE REVERSE FOR IMPORTANT INFORMATION

JUROR FEES: You will be paid $10.00 per day plus $0.15 per mile round trip from your house to the Courthouse for each day you are required to report for Jury Duty.

EMPLOYERS: Check with your employer to find out your company's policy regarding Jury Duty. If your employer requires proof of attendance, make sure to check the box on the 3 x 5 white card. Under Maine law a Juror's employment is protected. If you need more information contact the Clerk's office at 822-4106.

WHAT TO BRING: Make sure you bring the completed 3 x 5 card on the first day. Because of security reasons, no dangerous weapons, such as guns, knives and other potentially dangerous items such as knitting needles/hooks, scissors, leathermens or mace are allowed in the Courthouse.

LUNCH/SNACKS: Coffee, tea, hot chocolate are available in the Grand Jury Room. Soda and snack machines are on the second floor and basement floor of the building and there are many fine restaurants in the area.

DRESS CODE: You are asked to dress in an appropriate and dignified manner.

WHO CAN SERVE: Any US Citizen at least 18 years of age, and a resident of Cumberland County. There is no maximum age limit in the State of Maine.

WEATHER RELATED CLOSINGS: Cancellation notices will be broadcast on local television channels, WGME 13, WCSH 6, WMTW 8, and Radio station 101.9 by 6:00 am. School cancellation DOES NOT mean the Court will be closed.

PARKING & PARKING REIMBURSEMENT: Parking will be reimbursed through the payroll process, with a receipt, on the form provided by the court. However, the following lots will allow us to validate your parking ticket with no expense to you.

The Summons listed four area parking lots and driving Directions to the Courthouse.

FIRST DAY: Enter the Courthouse through the Newbury Street entrance (ground floor) and take the elevator to the 3rd floor, bare to the left as you exit the elevator through the hallway into the old part of the building. The Grand Jury Room is at the far end of the hallway, beyond the picture display of Judges. Please make yourself comfortable, if the Court Marshal is not present.

— — —

I think that as the Administrator of The Unified Maine Common Law Grand Jury I was Providentially summoned to serve on the Cumberland County Maine Grand Jury of my county and state.

— David E. Robinson
Brunswick, Maine

First Day

I appeared as summoned for Grand Jury Service on Monday morning, January 6, 2014, AT 8:30 AM at 205 Newbury Street, Portland, ME.

More than fifty people showed up at the Jury Room that day with the 3 x 5 inch attendance cards that came with their summons, and from this jury pool of respondents, <u>eighteen</u> Grand Jurists and <u>six</u> Grand Jurist Substitutes were drawn at random from all the cards which had been shuffled in a bowl; — 24 Grand Jurists in all. The rest of the people were excused and left.

Jurists seated on this Grand Jury for the next four months were:

1. **Joseph Henderson**
2. **David Robinson**
3. **Leslie Phelps**
4. **Philip Douglas**
5. **Christine Basbron**
6. **Melanie Maston**
7. **Brenda Endicot**
8. **Roland Spalding**
9. **Jason Putman**
10. **Keith Macavoy**
11. **Philip Paris**
12. **Diane Mankowsky**
13. **Diana Desovo**
14. **Gretchen French**
15. **Christopher Appleby**
16. **John Levine**
17. **Jeff Bowers**
18. **Kurt Marston**
19. **Ruth Wavy**
20. **Scott Tebo**
21. **James LaPators**
22. **Fredrick Bragdon**
23. **Larry Lasard**
24. **Paula French**

The Jurists were then told by the Clerk, *"Everyone Rise"* and **Judge Roland A. Cole** came into the Jury Room and administered our Oath.

Then **Judge Cole** appointed these four Grand Jury Officials:

Grand Jury Foreman:	**Kurt Marston**
Deputy Grand Jury Foreman:	**Paula French**
Grand Jury Clerk:	**Diane Mankowsky**
Grand Jury Doorkeeper:	**Christopher Appleby**

— — —

Judge Cole welcomed everyone there and told them that the Court Clerk would answer any questions that we might have. Then the judge excused himself and left the room.

The Court Clerk told the Jurists that the Grand Jury functions informally; that they were here to represent the General Public at large, and that all information pertaining to the cases that they would hear is to be held in confidence by the Jurists.

We the Grand Jurists then voted on 125 or so "Felony" Cases each week — "Yes" or "No" for indictment — by raised hands. After the Grand Jury Foreman had called for the vote, he would ask if there any were opposed, or if there were any abstentions. And the results of the votes were recorded in the file.

As Grand Jurists, we could ask any questions we wanted to ask and make any comments we wished to make when acting in confidence as the Grand Jury.

— — —

When the Grand Jury was seated and ready, a District Attorney waiting in the Hall would come into the Grand Jury Room with a stack of cases in hand — introduce himself of herself — and state the Name of the Accused as the Title of each Felony Case, and the number of offense Counts allegedly being charged and a little explanation about the charges, and then ask the Doorkeeper to tell the appropriate witness to come in.

The witness would come in and be asked by the grand jury

foreman to "swear or affirm" to "tell the truth". The witness would then be asked to be seated and present his case.

After the witness had presented his case, the district attorney would then ask the grand jurists if they had any questions for the witness or himself. Then, after the grand jurists's questions had been answered, and resolved to their satisfaction, the prosecutor and his witness would leave the grand jury room, so the jurists could discuss the case in private and vote on whether or not there was "probable cause" for an indictment to be filed against the accused.

After the vote was taken and recorded in the paper work, the doorkeeper would call the prosecutor back into the jury room to receive the results of the jurists's raised hand vote. The grand jury foreman and the secretary would assist the district attorney with any other paperwork required.

The prosecutor would then leave the jury room; and the doorman would call for the next case.

Then, this "due process" pattern would repeat.

Each case was generally allotted 15 to 30 minutes or so, or occasionally longer times, as required.

This grand jury process is a closed secret process engaged in hearing and deciding felony cases for probable cause and require a majority of 13 votes to Indict for further petite jury trial. $(2/3 \times 18 = 12 + 1 = 13)$

Felony cases are graduated as A, B or C according to the number of offense counts per case. A prior civil offense becomes a felony if and when it is repeated for a second time.

— — —

Prosecutors

In Cumberland County, there is <u>one</u> District Attorney; <u>one</u> Deputy District Attorney; and <u>thirteen</u> Assistant District Attorneys employed by the court.

1. **Stephanie Anderson**, District Attorney
2. **Margaret Elam** [Meg], Deputy District Attorney

Assistant District Attorneys:
1. **LeaAnne Sutton**
2. **Kate Tierney**
3. **Anne Berlind**
4. **Tracy Gorham**
5. **Debora Chnielewski**
6. **Jennifer Ackerman**
7. **Mathew Tice**
8. **Julia Sheridan**
9. **Michael Madigan**
10. **Robert Ellis** [Bud]
11. **William Barry**
12. **Hannah May**
13. **Angela Cannon** [Angie]

The Jurisdictions of the Cumberland County Prosecuting Attorneys cover the following five Classifications of felony:

Class 1. **<u>Juvenile Unit</u>**
Class 2. **<u>Red</u>:** - Windham / West Brunswick / Freeport
Class 3. **<u>Purple</u>:** - Portland / Falmouth / Railroad
Class 4. **<u>Blue</u>:** - Maine State Police / South Portland / Scarborough / Sheriffs Department
Class 5. **<u>Domestic Violence</u>**

Comment Aside

This experience is and has been for me Providential. I doubt that anyone knew before that I am the volunteer founder and Administrator of the Unified Maine Common Law Grand Jury for the Maine Republic Free State, — and the State Organizer for the Common Law Grand Juries in all of the 16 Counties in Maine.

I shared several of the "Common Law Handbook For Juror's, Sheriff's, Bailiff's, and Justices's" and one or two with the Prosecutors. I am now offering a Five Booklet Set for use in the public domain at this time.

I am gathering information for the other Counties of the State to coordinate with the National Liberty Alliance of which I am a part — http://nationallibertyalliance.org

— David E. Robinson
Brunswick, Maine

Last Day — Shock!

I really don't know what to say . . .

The last day of my experience serving on the Cumberland County Maine Grand Jury, proceeded as usual without incident, until we were presented with our final and last case, whereupon I totally lost it, excused myself, and quickly left the room.

— — —

Prior to this final case we had been presented with rather common, ordinary cases, such as driving without a driver license; speeding on the highways; domestic violence; assault on some person; theft of public or private property; shoplifting; and so forth.

And a few of the cases were extraordinary, such as sexual contact with a child; soliciting prostitution; or attempted murder.

But the *last* case was — if I remember correctly before I lost it — failure to file a 1040 Income tax form and failure to pay the so-called "individual income tax" on the alleged felon's "income".

As grand jurors we were being asked — **not** to either convict or set free the accused — but to simply determine if the arresting officer had probable cause to make the arrest, — and to GIVE THE COURT OUR PERMISSION — as the people of Maine — for the court to proceed. No big deal. It happens all the time.

But with the fraudulent IRS, it was a different story. I was prejudiced because a friend of mine and I had sued the IRS for good cause, and our case had been, I think, dismissed for some procedural mistake.

In the hall, outside of the jury room, I confided to the Marshal on duty there, that I knew that the IRS is a fraud and why.

However: I didn't realize the full extent of the shocking state of mind this put me in, until halfway back to Brunswick, near Freeport, it hit me again and I just had to turn around and return to the court, and confess my crime of not hearing what the IRS agent was going to say to my friends, there in the grand jury room.

I think it's a serious crime to withhold evidence of a crime when you are aware of a particular crime.

And yet, to expose my friends to what I have learned in this regard, would be a shock to them that I could not bear, so in disregard of the person being charged, I cowardly excused myself and fled the scene.

I thought that if I returned to the court and confessed my crime it could make a difference, but by the time I had returned to the courthouse it was all of no avail.

The clerk at the window of the grand jury clerk's office kindly re-assured me that although I was very upset, the individual who had been charged with the felony would now go to trial and have the right to be defended there.

The clerk told me to not to feel guilty, to go home and be at peace, and that all was not lost.

I realize now that I had done the right thing.

It would not have been wise to get into a verbal debate with the IRS at that time, because the IRS agent might not be aware of the fraud perpetrated by the IRS.

And it goes much deeper than that . . .

Treachery & Deception with words

After the Civil War, the federal Government <u>simulated</u> (counterfeited) the <u>original</u> political status our forefathers founded for us into a <u>second class</u> political status created for the black man to give him <u>political status</u> as opposed to being <u>property of the state</u>.

They took the black man off the <u>southern</u> plantation and put him on the <u>federal</u> plantation with civil rights.

Hence, the <u>simulation</u> we are living out today where we think that when we say "<u>I am a citizen of the United States</u>" it means the <u>original</u> political status with <u>Constitutional protections</u> (*not Constitutional rights because our Rights come from God*) protected by the Constitution. But it does not.

— — —

The Bait & Switch

Few Americans know that <u>two forms of citizenship exist</u> in the United States.

1) "<u>citizens of the United States</u>" under Congress.
2) "<u>citizens of the States United</u>" under the Constitution.

1) "<u>US citizen residents</u>" (citizens of the United States) and
2) "<u>US alien nationals</u>" (aliens of the United States).

In other words, <u>resident *US citizens*</u>, and <u>national *US aliens*</u>.

And a *<u>US citizen</u>* can change his status to a *<u>US national</u>* via a *<u>legal declaration</u>*.

Voluntary Servitude in America

Ask yourself: <u>What is my status in society</u>? Am I a <u>slave</u> in servitude to a master or am I a <u>free man</u> whose body and assets are **not** owned or controlled by any outside force?

Am I a <u>slave</u>, a <u>serf</u>, or a <u>free man</u>?

We are <u>federal second-class-citizens</u> who have relinquished many or our liberties and constitutional rights. NOT according to the vision of our Forefathers of their day.

The gradual loss of our liberties and rights began <u>after</u> the <u>War between the States</u> and the <u>14th Amendment</u>, and accelerated during the Great Depression and bankruptcy of the United States in the 1930's, when American citizens unwittingly contracted to replace their status as free men with that of an inferior, second-class citizens under the 14th Amendment.

Over time, the federal Government gradually usurped most of the power that had been constitutionally granted by the People to the States.

<u>State</u> Primacy became <u>Federal</u> Primacy.

<u>State citizenship</u> was usurped by the federal Government when <u>United States citizenship</u> was established thereon.

Americans unwittingly, and supposedly voluntarily, accepted <u>federal US Government jurisdiction</u> over their lives, by willingly declaring that they were "<u>citizens of the United States</u>"; instead of "<u>sovereigns of the States United</u>".

They declared it for their children and themselves, on their birth certificates;

They declared it when they filed their taxes;

They declared it on their passports; bank accounts; driver licences;— and so forth.

When you declare yourself to be a "citizens of the United States" you contract with and enter into the inferior legal status of second-class citizenship. Once you have done so, you become subject to the many regulations, policies and laws — most of which do not apply to State citizens — because under the Constitution as it existed prior to the 14th Amendment the Federal government lacked the constitutional jurisdiction to reach State citizens except under the limited enumerated powers delegated to it by the several States of the Union.

The 14th Amendment gave the Federal government virtually unlimited power and jurisdiction over its newly created second-class US citizens ("citizens of the United States"; instead of "citizens of the States United).

There are three important legal and political written and verbal land-mines that you must learn about on your road to freedom.

1) the new US "citizen"; 2) the new US "resident"; and 3) the new US "jurisdiction" called the "United States" — as opposed to the "States United" in the Union under the U.S. Constitution.

These three terms lie at the very heart of the Federal government's introduction of feudal law into our Nation — the very same feudal law that our Forebears shed their blood to banish forever from this Land and from their posterity.

We Americans have existed for decades in a form of bondage that is foreign to the American way of life, in violation of the trembling sense of freedom that exists in the hearts and souls of Americans.

We're right back where we started from in 1776, when Thomas Jefferson stated in the Declaration of Independence, speaking about King George III of England:

> *He has combined with others to subject us to a jurisdiction foreign to our constitution, and unacknowledged by our laws.*

The feudal law jurisdiction imposed upon us today is, likewise, foreign to our Constitution.

How willing are you to learn correctly how to claim your new/old/citizen status and remove yourself from the jurisdiction of a government that guards its power jealously to itself and seriously?

Knowledge is power, and there is power in numbers. In the end, even the most powerful governments fail when facing the wrath of the people.

Many Americans would knowingly choose to remain Federal citizens (US citizenship) to receive the myriad of protective benefits in exchange for their freedom. But many more would NOT — if offered a choice.

We Americans have unwittingly volunteered into federal bondage; where a fraud has been perpetrated that must be addressed. The fraud lies in the execution of a contract, without the disclosure of its true intent.

> *Fraud is using deception in order to induce another to part with property or surrender some legal right and the parting with property or surrendering some legal right occurs.* — Landmark Dev. Group v. Tmk Assocs., 2001 Conn. Supe. LEXIZ 731 (Conn. Super. Ct. Mar. 5, 2002).

> *Fraud destroys the validity of everything into which it enters. It vitiates the most solemn contracts, documents, and even judgments.* — Intl. Milling Col. v. Priem., 179 Wis. 622 (Wis. 1923).

My withheld Testimony - part 1

The IRS is the biggest lie and scam in world history.

I.R.S. -- the three most frightening and loathed letters in the English language. This deep-seated fear and loathing serves a very specific purpose. It serves to keep the People of America enslaved in submission to an illusion; a lie. It is an emotional and psychological chain around the neck of the American people.

The IRS has a horrible reputation; it has by its own admission committed crimes against innocent citizens and continues to be the "Gestapo of America" today.

They confiscate more homes, destroy more families, take more money, ruin more lives, and commit more crimes than all the street gangs combined.

The IRS is a private debt collection agency for the non-federal Federal Reserve Bank, under Title 15 of the U.S Code.

The IRS is **not** a government agency. The IRS was formerly the Bureau of Internal Revenue (BIR) situated in and with authority only in the Philippine Islands (Trust Fund # 61) and Puerto Rico (Trust Fund # 62).

In the 1950's with the stroke of the pen the BIR was transformed into the current, notorious IRS and brought over **onto** the 50 united States.

This was done without any Congressional authority. There is no Congressional authority recorded anywhere in any law books for the IRS to exist and operate in the 50 states of the Union.

Most Americans do not realize that there are two Title's 26.

Title 26 United States Code and Title 26 Internal Revenue Code

Title 26 Internal Revenue Code is the <u>Debt Collection Manual</u> for the IRS.

This Manual has nothing to do with Constitutional Rights because the IRS does not collect an "income tax". The IRS simply collects a "user fee" payable to the Federal Reserve Bank because we Americans are using its *private credit* system.

The "user fee" had to be disguised as an "income tax" to fool the American people and keep us enslaved.

Title 26 United States Code is "non-positive law" which means that no "American Citizen" is subject to it. However, all "U.S. citizens" **are** subject to it.

In order to understand "U.S. citizen" you must go to 28 USC 3002.

Most "American Citizens" have perhaps *unknowingly,* but *voluntarily,* surrendered their Sovereignty in exchange for the "immunities and privileges" of the 14th Amendment.

There are literally hundreds of unilateral, silent contracts by which American Citizens *declare themselves* to be "U.S. citizens" -- meaning "citizens of the United States" -- and thus subject to *both* Titles 26.

By *voluntarily* becoming a "U.S. citizen" every "American Citizen" declares him/herself to be an "indentured servant" (slave) to the non-federal Federal Reserve Bank, with no Constitutional Rights, whatsoever.

Title 26 USC is a *private law* that applies only to "U.S. corporate citizens", who are *all* viewed as *employees* of the corporate United States identified at 28 USC 3002(15)(A)(B)(C).

(15) "United States" means—

(A) a Federal corporation;

(B) an agency, department, com-mission, board, or other entity of the United States; or

(C) an instrumentality of the United States.

i.e.: The "United States" is a Federal corporation of the "United States".

The Federal Reserve Banking system is **not** a Federal government agency, there aren't "reserves", and there is **no** real *"money of account of the United States"* in existence or in use in the United States today.

The Federal Reserve Banking system is a *private cartel* that has usurped the authority of the Congress to coin Money.

Starting from 1913, we Americans *voluntarily* submitted to this private law through our own ignorance. Once we submitted to this "private contract law" we became voluntary slaves of the Federal Reserve System and the IRS.

This was a silent *coup d'e-tat* wherein the American People unknowingly became the slaves of the Federal Reserve Bank.

The "Killing Blow", the *coup de grace* [pronounced, 'de gra'], was delivered upon the American People by Franklin D. Roosevelt in 1933 when he removed the Gold Standard from the American economy. Since 1933, no American Citizen has actually "paid" for anything, we have just "exchanged" worthless Federal Reserve Notes for more worthless Federal Reserve Notes.

Since 1933 **no** American has owned their property in Allodium. This is why the "STATE OF [your STATE]" can take your property for just about any reason; i.e eminent domain; failure to pay so-called "property taxes"; state income taxes; etc.

IRS authority is applicable **solely** to government agencies and personnel by 26 USC 6331(a):

> **"Levy may be made upon the accrued salary or wages of any officer, employee, or elected official, of the United States, the District of Columbia, or any agency or instrumentality of the United States or the District of Columbia, by serving a notice of levy on the employer."**

First, such notices must include a Form 668B, which is the actual levy.

Second, only those large businesses and governmental units that have designated officers and written agreements are authorized to receive notices of levy by mail.

Third, to complete the levy, another form, Form 668C, must be served but cannot be served by mail; it must be served in person. This completes service of "notice of levy".

Absent Form 668B there is no evidence that there is a levy. In the event the IRS fails to serve either or both the levy and Form 668C, service of process is incomplete and the IRS is in default.

In brief, there can be no seizure before a judgment is rendered in a state court.

The INTERNAL REVENUE SERVICE is incorporated in Delaware as a collection agency for a Puerto Rico Company titled "INTERNAL REVENUE TAX AND AUDIT SERVICE" (IRS) -- For Profit General Corporation -- Incorporated date 7/12/33 -- File No.0325720.

Therefore, the "INTERNAL REVENUE SERVICE" must be recognized in its lawful status as a "debt collection agency" accountable under 15 USC 1692e.

A debt collector may not use false, deceptive or misleading representation.

It is a common misconception that the "INTERNAL REVENUE SERVICE" is part of the United States Government, but in fact, it is a "Private for-profit Business Corporation".

Through fraud; manipulation; conspiracy; deceit; and impersonation of law enforcement personnel; the IRS has become an "Organized Crime Syndicate" operating illegally in every State of this Union.

There are five major elements of this Puerto Rican Organized 'RECO' Crime:

1. "Extortionate Credit Transactions" (18 USC 891-894)

2. "Conspiracy Against Rights" (18 USC 241)

3. "Extortion" (18 USC 1001)

4. "Seizure of Property without Due Process" — Violation of 4th Amendment

5. "Seizure of bank accounts/ income without due process" — Violation 4th Amendment

The IRS is fraudulently operating under the designation of the "DEPARTMENT OF THE TREASURY". As a corporation, the IRS cannot lawfully misrepresent itself to the public by declaring itself to be a part of government. This act is prohibited by 15 USC 1692e.

The IRS is clearly engaged in conspiracy to defraud the public by leading the public to believe they are a part of government.

Our "United States Representatives" are responsible to stop this "Organized Crime" and to date have remained silent. When criminals are engaged in "Organized Crime" and doing so under fraudulent authority by declaring themselves to be the government, when in fact they are not, they are causing the people to despise their government and judge it by the conduct of the "IRS Agents".

All "IRS Agents" are lawfully challenged as "Foreign Agents" under 22 USC 611. They have no authority of law other than that of a debt collector under Title 15 of the United States Code.

The chief IRS weapon is *fear*. Fear is the best weapon they have, to, in effect, *compel* people to "voluntarily comply".

The IRS has no lawful authority to assess you with a Subtitle A income tax liability, because the only "person" who can create such a liability *by assessing you* — is you.

You can prosecute these same agents for malfeasance; conspiracy against rights; constructive fraud; obstruction of justice; racketeering; mail fraud mailing threatening communications; and several other crimes.

Be an informed Citizen; a pro per litigant; informed voter and juror. Know your rights and understand the law.

'Knowledge will forever govern ignorance; and a people who mean to be their own governors must arm themselves with the power which knowledge gives." — *author withheld.*

Our "Ancient Principles" need to be revived. They refer to the Ten Commandments and the Common Law. The Common Law in simple terms is common sense that has its roots in the Ten Commandments which have been left **out** of government schools.

My withheld Testimony - part 2

Many have heard the <u>battle cry</u> of the tax warriors of today: <u>Show me the Law</u> (regarding the <u>individual income tax claims</u> of the IRS) believing that no such law exists. And when the IRS won't <u>Show me the Law</u> we think that they do not have one; <u>but they do</u>!

They won't <u>Show me the Law</u> because it would expose their entire, gigantic, deceitful, fraudulent con game! They don't want people to know which law supposedly locks them into the individual income tax because they might see how the system is set-up and remove themselves from the oppressive jurisdiction and control of the IRS.

<u>The Law</u> requiring a <u>citizen</u> (a corporation) to pay an income tax is <u>26 CFR 1.1-1(a) and 1.1-1(c)</u>.

<u>Section (c) above</u>: "Every <u>person</u> (corporation) born or naturalized in the <u>United States</u> and subject to its jurisdiction is a <u>citizen</u> (corporation)."

i.e.: A <u>citizen</u> required to pay an income tax is every <u>person</u> subject to the jurisdiction of the <u>United States</u>.

i.e.: A <u>person</u> required to pay an income tax is every <u>citizen of the United States</u>.

(In the eyes of the IRS both a <u>person</u> and a <u>citizen of the United States</u> is a <u>corporation</u>).

i.e.: A "<u>citizen of the United States</u>" is a "<u>person</u>" seen in the eyes of the IRS as a "<u>corporation</u>" required to pay an income tax.

Therefore, when you claim to be a "<u>citizen of the United States</u>" you are seen in the eyes of the IRS and the U.S. Government as a "<u>person</u>" or "<u>corporation</u>" required to pay an "<u>income</u>" tax.

The rest of the entire IRS code is used for determining HOW MUCH the resulting "<u>tax payer</u>" owes.

— — —

The Law presented in 26 CFR is from Title 26 of the Code of Federal Regulations. Federal Regulations are NOT laws, although often referred to as "little laws", they are regulations.

Title 26 of the Code of Federal Regulations regulates Title 26 of the Internal Revenue Code which are the laws regarding the individual income tax requirements of the IRS.

— 26 CFR regulates 26 IRC —

Title 26 IRC is NOT substantiated law. 26 IRC was passed by the House of Representatives as a House Resolution ONLY. 26 IRC was not even *voted on* by the Senate let alone *passed* by the Senate; 26 IRC was *not even signed* by the President.

The House of Representatives has jurisdiction only over the District of Columbia and the territories (the federal zone) i.e. the Corporate United States (as distinct from the United States of America), and NOT over any of the Union States.

The IRS only applies to federal citizens who have duties and privileges (not rights) under the 14th Amendment and are called "citizens of the United States". (small "c")

If you are one of those 'persons' (corporations) (citizens of the United States) just pay the tax and don't complain!

But if you are NOT one of those 'persons' (corporations) (citizens of the United States) you are a U.S. National, a non-resident alien of the corporate United States as defined at <u>26 USC 7701(b)(1)(B)</u> who is being defrauded by the IRS.

All individuals in America who declare themselves to be "citizens of the United States" are presumed to have declared that they voluntarily place themselves under the feudal law jurisdiction of the Federal Government and have pledged their bodies, their assets, their minor children and their labor to the federal government as 2nd Class citizens.

A corrective Affidavit presented to the IRS is the linchpin of Government tyranny and control.

Our collective enslavement is due to our ignorance of the tactics and techniques of our federal Government and the IRS!

"My people are destroyed for lack of knowledge." *(Hosea 4:6).*

The term 'resident' of the United States is a rebuttable presumption. All that is necessary in a court setting is to state clearly and unequivocally, "I rebut the presumption that I am a 'resident' of the United States" and provide some properly executed corrective Affidavit stating that you are rebutting the presumption. Such as:

"I am not that 'person' (corporation/strawman). The 14th Amendment offers me no rights, so I owe no correlative duties to the IRS. This statutory regulation does not apply to me. I demand my true and correct civil and political status as a natural born citizen under the original Constitution of the United States of America; NOT under the bylaws of the corporate federal United States."

NOTE: Before the incorporation of the United States, State Citizens considered their Country to be their respective State.

Now (ever since the incorporation of the United States) new deal lawyers do not hesitate to assert that private citizens *can unknowingly* contract away their constitutional rights.

Through this technique of *government by contract* they have broken down State lines and invaded the people's private affairs.

As a result: slaves cannot own property; slaves ARE property.

The Civil War was set up by the Rothschild Brothers. One brother financed the North. Another brother financed the South.

Contrary to popular revised history, that war was not fought over slavery, at least not initially. Now to say that those responsible did not have this plan in mind is another question, but publicly it was initiated over taxation; the Industrial North v. the Agrarian South.

Our taxes were constitutional at that time and consisted of imposts and excises mandated by the Constitution.

The southern planters were paying the majority of the taxes, as they were doing most of the trade with England. They therefore were bearing most of the tax burden while the Industrial North benefited by producing and selling domestically and not bearing much, if any, of the taxation burden.

The genius of the Civil War.

Halfway through this horrid war, Lincoln put forth his ideas in his Emancipation Proclamation. It was only at that time that the slavery issue became a public cause. It was by no accident that the opening salvos of the Civil were fired at Fort Sumter, South Carolina. That was one of the main ports where the taxes of the Southern trade were imposed.

After the war, there were some four million former slaves, now call freed men, running around the countryside. As stated plainly in the language and wording of the *Slaughter-House Cases,* in most instances the freed men no longer had the care and protection of their former owners. They had legally been 'things', the 'objects' of someone's property rights; but that condition no longer applied.

They had to be given not only some form of political status but civil status as well. To accomplish this, the 14th Amendment was forced through the various state legislatures. In fact, if the southern states would not pass that piece of legislation, their legislators were run-off and more cooperative legislators were put in their place. They also burned many important law libraries in the South whenever a State refused to pass that amendment.

The new form of citizenship, "citizen of the United States", was secondary and subservient to the original citizenship "Citizen of one's State" that had been clearly established and understood since the founding of the Republic.

As you can read in both Congressmen Traficant and McFadden's public statements in the Congressional Record, the traitorous *de facto* Federal Reserve prompted government agents to set up a system wherein you were allowed to volunteer into the servitude of a second class citizenship originally instituted for the recently freed Southern Negro slaves.

The only problem is that THEY DID NOT disclose these changes in political and civil status to the people hence the Fraud.

Therefore, our access to our original God-given constitutionally protected original Rights, secured by the blood and treasure of our forefathers, was effectively cut off and destroyed.

Federal citizenship, first and State citizenship, second *if* you 'reside' instead of being domiciled within a state.

THIS IS FRAUD! THIS IS TREASON! If enough Americans become aware of this information and exercise their God-given birthright this con game can be stopped! That is, if you want it to and have the political and patriotic will to take action and MAKE IT HAPPEN!

The entire process starts with you.

Some Background

In 1776 we came out of BONDAGE with FAITH, UNDER-STANDING and COURAGE. Even against great odds and with much bloodshed, we battled our way to achieve LIBERTY.

LIBERTY is that delicate balance between the force of government and the FREE WILL of man.

To be a good master you must always remember the true "pecking order" or chain of command in this nation:

1. GOD created man;
2. Man created the Constitution;
3. The Constitution created Government;
4. Government created Corporations, etc.

The base of power was to remain in WE THE PEOPLE but unfortunately, it was lost to those leaders acting in the name of the government, such as politicians, bureaucrats, judges, lawyers, etc.

As a result America is now functioning like a democracy instead of the REPUBLIC it is meant to be. A democracy is dangerous because it is a *one-vote system* as opposed to a Republic which is a *three-vote system:* Three votes to check tyranny, not just one. American citizens have not been informed of *their other two votes.*

Our first vote is at the polls on election-day when we pick those who are to represent us in the seats of government. But what can be done if those elected officials just don't perform as promised or expected? Well, *the second two votes* are the most effective means by which the common people of any nation on earth have, even had, in controlling those appointed to serve them in government.

The second vote comes when you serve on a Grand Jury. Before anyone can be brought to trial for a capital or infamous crime by those acting in the name of the government, permission to act must be obtained from people serving on the Grand Jury!

The third vote is the most powerful: this is **when you are acting as a jury member yourself** during a courtroom trial. At this point, "the buck stops" with YOU!

In this setting EACH JUROR HAS MORE POWER than the President of the United States, all of Congress, and all of the judges combined into one!!!

At the time of adoption of the Constitution, the jury's role , as a defense against political oppression, was unquestioned in American jurisprudence. This nation survived until the 1850's when prosecutions under the Fugitive Slave Act were largely unsuccessful because juries refused to convict the accused.

Then judges began to *erode* the institution of free juries, leading to the *absurd compromise* that is the current state of the law. While our courts uniformly state that juries have the power to return a verdict of not guilty, whatever the facts my be, they often routinely tell jurors *just the opposite.*

The community should educate itself. Then citizens called for jury duty could teach the judges a needed lesson in Civics. One of the important ways our nation's founders provided to insure that *you, not the growing army of politicians, judges, lawyers, and bureaucrats, rule this nation.*

The lesson focuses on *the rule of power that you possess* as a JUROR, how you got it, why you have it, and remind you of the basis on which you must decide not only the facts placed in evidence but also the validity and applicability of every law, rule, regulation, ordinance, or instruction given by any man seated as a district judge or attorney when you serve as a **JUROR.**

One JUROR can stop tyranny with a "NOT GUILTILY VOTE!" The only power the judge has over the JURY is their ignorance!

The federal income tax is voluntary.

Steve Miller, former Director of the Internal Revenue Service (IRS) admitted recently at a Congressional hearing, that the "taxes" collected by the IRS are not *mandatory,* but voluntary.

While the government has constitutional authority to tax, the IRS has engaged in "unlawful, unconstitutional, unfair and biased" debt collection practices to declare salaries and wages to be "income" without any legal basis.

The definition of "income" *excludes* wages, salaries and tips.

Black's Law Dictionary defines "income tax" as being "a tax on the yearly profits arising from property, professions, trades and offices."

Based on this and other references, wages are not "profits" but are instead the simple exchange of labor for money. While businesses frequently pay taxes on their "profits", they do not pay taxes on their "expenses".

The labor of an individual is the "expense" required to obtain the so-called "money" received, therefore it is *not* "profit."

Income must have the essential feature of "gain" to the recipient.

This was true when the 16th amendment became effective. If there is no "gain" there is no "income". Income is not synonymous with "receipts".

Reasonable compensation for labor or services rendered is *not* "profit". It is a clean and simple *quid quo pro* (equal value for equal value) exchange.

You and the IRS's Deceit

Most Americans unknowingly made an "election" to pay the Federal Income Tax, *unaware* of their option to not do so.

Most Americans made what is called a "statutory election" during their working lives, by declaring that they are "citizens of the United States" (the federal zone) and filing federal income tax returns. This tax has been accepted by us as the norm, without us knowing the law.

The US Supreme Court decision *United States v. Erie Railroad Co., 106 US 327 (1882)* stated that:

> *"The power of the United States to tax is limited to persons, property, and businesses within their jurisdiction, as much as that of a State is limited to the same subjects within its jurisdiction."*

In other words:

> *"The power of the Federal Government to tax is limited to statutory legal fictions per 26 USC §7701(a)(1), property, and businesses within the jurisdiction of the District of Columbia United States as much as that 'power' of a State is limited to the same subjects within the District of Columbia's federal jurisdiction."*

Chief Justice Marshall in *McCulloch v. Maryland, 4 Wheat, 316, 428* stated:

> *"All subjects over which the power of the State (the Federal Government) extends are objects of taxation, but those (subjects) over which it does not extend (people the Union States) are, upon the soundest principles, <u>exempt from taxation</u>."*

So, the power of the Federal Government is limited to *statutory legal fictions* called persons; property; and businesses; within the District of Columbia — which are subjects or objects of taxation.

Most Americans erroneously think this includes them as subjects of taxation, but it does not.

Chief Justice Marshall stated:

"...but those over which it (the power of the Federal Government) does not extend, are, upon the soundest principles, <u>exempt from taxation</u>".

So there are those people who are exempt from Taxation!

Those people who are exempt from Taxation must be those born in the 50 states of the Union, or why would he have so stated it?

Most Americans are **not** statutory legal fictions, property of, or engage in a business in the District of Columbia.

But maybe the National Government sees us as such!!!

But how did that happen? Did somebody lie to you?

It is a federal crime for Americans to lie to a federal officer even if not under oath. But it is **not** a federal crime for a federal officer to lie to the American Public!

This is their way to impose criminal liability, even when a federal prosecutor can't prove any other crime. Lying got Martha Stewart and others into hot water with the IRS.

Those in the Federal Government can lie to the American Public without any repercussions. And they **do** lie. It's called Propaganda, or withholding the truth.

The techniques of propaganda have been used by the Federal Government for more than a century to support their suppositions.

Well, the Federal Income Tax (FIT) **is** lawful and legal. But you were **not** told that the FIT is applicable only to *four select groups:* statutory "tax payers" defined at 26 USC §7701(a)(14).

<u>First liable group</u>: **Public Officials** who work for the Federal Government.

Second liable group: **Resident Aliens** from other countries who moved to the 50 states of the Union, or to the District of Columbia to live and work.

Third liable group: **American Nationals** who were born in one of the 50 states of the Union who moved to and reside in one of the Federal Territories such as Puerto Rico, American Samoa, and the US Virgin Islands, etc.

Fourth liable group: **American Nationals** who have made a statutory "election" ("choice") to have their income treated like that of a US Resident Alien (group two). This fourth group is by far the largest of all people who are "statutory tax payers".

So American Nationals who did **not** "elect" ("chose") to have their income treated like that of a US Resident Alien **do not have to file an FIT return**.

In other words, American Nationals who did **not** "elect" to be treated like a US Resident Alien are "Nonresident Aliens" of the District United States (Washington, D.C.) **who do not have to file a Federal Income Tax return**.

The Federal Government tells you this in the Internal Revenue Code, but in an obtuse and confusing way.

The term "Nonresident Alien" does not even remotely sound like a reference to those born in the 50 states of the Union, or Americans trying to make a living in the private sector of the United States, meaning the 50 states of the Union.

The US Congress defines a "Nonresident Alien" by **who he is not** — instead of by who he is.

According to the Internal Revenue Code:

> *"An individual is a Nonresident Alien if such individual is neither a citizen of the United States nor a resident of the United States."*
>
> *— 26 USC 7701(b)(1)(B).*

Therefore a "Nonresident Alien" is an American National who has **not** become a citizen, nor a resident of the District of Columbia Federal United States.

"A statutory US citizen is a person (a legal fiction) legislatively born (created by the US Congress) in the statutory United States (the District of Columbia) and subject to thereof" (US citizens are under the dominion and control of the Federal Government).

The *statutory definition* of US citizen does not mean the same thing as the *constitutional definition* of US Citizen referred to in the Constitution of the United States of American; ratified in 1791. **They are two different types of citizen.**

Former President of the United States Franklin D. Roosevelt stated that: *"Governments never do anything by accident, if government does something, you can bet it was carefully planned."*

So defining an American National as ***not being a Resident Alien*** instead of as a Nonresident Alien, was no accidental mistake on the part of Congress.

According to Roosevelt, the definition created by Congress was a *purposeful act of deception* to hide its real meaning.

A Nonresident Alien is an American National who did **not** voluntarily "elect" to file a Federal Income Tax return.

ONCE AGAIN - TO BE CLEAR:
A "Nonresident Alien" is an "American National".

An "American National" has no FIT (federal income tax) liability — UNLESS he makes an "election" to have his income taxed like that of a US Resident Alien; a foreigner from another country who lives and works in the Constitutional Republic or in the District of Columbia United States.

However: You *unknowingly* confirm that "election" whenever you declare, or admit, on any government form, that:
"I am a 'citizen of the United States'."

See Appendix for
"Revocation of Election" letter to the IRS

Honoring Oaths

It seems that many of those who make and interpret our laws have little regard for their oaths to preserve, protect and defend our original United States Constitution.

Consider the ruling by the United States Supreme Court in the *Slaughter-House Cases* in 1873.

These cases involved <u>state citizens</u> who were seeking relief from <u>federal jurisdiction</u> on a state issue. The Federal Supreme Court reaffirmed <u>the primacy of the state issue</u> and the privileges and immunities <u>of the natural born citizen of the state</u> — not of the 14th Amendment Federal citizens.

The <u>private state citizens</u> were sent to their State for relief. But today, we are <u>federal</u> US citizens instead. Here's what the court said:

> *Of the privileges and immunities of the <u>citizens</u> <u>of the United States</u>, and of the privileges and immunities of the <u>Citizens of a State</u>...it is only former — <u>citizens of the United States</u> — which are placed by the clause — <u>the second clause of the 14th Amendment</u> — under the protection of the Federal constitution, and that the latter — <u>the Citizens of a State</u>, — whatever they may be, are not intended to have any additional protection by this paragraph of the Amendment ... the latter — <u>the Citizens of a State</u> — must rest for their security and protection where they have heretofore rested, for <u>they are not embraced by this paragraph of the Amendment</u>.*

But with...exceptions...few...the entire domain of the privileges and immunities of <u>Citizens of the State</u>, as above defined, <u>lay within the constitutional and legislative power of the State</u> and <u>without that of the Federal Government</u>. Was it the purpose of the 14th Amendment ... <u>to transfer</u> the security and protection of all the civil rights which we have mentioned <u>from the State to the Federal government</u>? And...was it intended to bring within the power of Congress the entire domain of civil rights heretofore belonging exclusively to the States? [NO.]

With few exceptions, <u>state citizens</u> worked within the state where they lived, as the federal government had no jurisdiction <u>over state citizens or state issues</u>.

Its jurisdiction was over the <u>14th Amendment federal citizen</u>, and that citizenship was limited to the slaves who had been freed by the 13th Amendment.

All governments evolve. <u>Representative Republics</u>, such as ours, which restrict federal power, <u>become democracies</u>, then <u>socialistic</u>, and as history demonstrates, <u>ultimately fail</u>. The average Republic exist for 200 years. And the time of its failure, looks nothing like the original protective contract executed by the states/the people. This is an historical, empirical truth.

Political Status in the United States

The method used by the <u>federal</u> government to deceive its own people, and take over the freest county in the history of the world, and turn it into a land of confused <u>legal slaves</u>, can be found in the <u>federal passport application</u> issued by the <u>US Department of State</u> (DOS). A means by which to teach this complicated and complex legal information.

There are <u>two distinctly different types of political status</u> — or citizenship if you will — in the United States. And this application form gives one an <u>official document</u> by which to show to anyone, who is willing to listen and think outside of the box, <u>the truth that is stranger than fiction</u>.

The United States is only the second country in the history of the world where man has been able to exercise his God-given Natural Rights.

We have been collectively tricked out of those Rights by the bait and switch and been placed into legalized bondage and slavery.

Legally, you are an asset owned and pledged to the federal government. <u>International bankers own and control you as property and collateral in their bogus paper money schemes</u>.

If that doesn't make you mad, and send chills up and down you spine, you may not be the person who is supposed to be reading this report.

Many are called, but few are chosen, to take part in this great endeavor, <u>to speak the truth</u> to those having ears to hear.

The big secret is that <u>we have been enslaved</u> and totally controlled by a network of regulatory agencies such as the IRS, <u>through the treachery of words</u>.

I will demonstrate this treachery to you by using the single most important informational gathering form which allows you to inform the government of the nature and state of your national citizenship.

Remember, All matters having to do with citizenship are decided by the U.S. Department of State (DOS).

An entire nation of free men and women has been converted to federal feudal slaves under the exact same form of slavery that governed most of Europe and England for nearly 1000 years.

For years people have said: "There are two sets of laws, one for them and one for use." This is true today.

A U.S. Passport is the single most important document in the entire arsenal of federal government identification documents. It not only serves to identify you, but also to set forth your legal status and personality.

On it two, distinct, legal statuses, are listed.

"Study to show yourself approved"

1. http://tinyurl.com/kgstsw9
2. http://tinyurl.com/n7xccyb
3. http://tinyurl.com/loun4df
4. http://tinyurl.com/mwnzspe
5. http://tinyurl.com/axxv5jq
6. http://tinyurl.com/m2yy2hl
7. http://tinyurl.com/lfnv9kb
8. http://tinyurl.com/ly99w7j
9. http://tinyurl.com/loa34qa
10. http://tinyurl.com/lqnrz9g

Rights v. Privileges

Rights are given by God. Privileges are given by man — and can easily be altered, changes or taken away by man. These privileges —now called "civil rights" — have replaced your God-given Rights, here in the corporate United States.

This was accomplished by your unconscious act of legally asking for it to be so.

When asked *"are you a citizen of the United States?"* or *"are you a resident of the United States?"* you answered or signified *"Yes"*.

Our rulers have thusly tricked you into specifying a special and specific political status where you have presumably accepted privileges called "civil rights" which automatically replaced your natural, God-given Rights — in their presumed opinion.

Under our system of law, *"Ignorance of the law is no excuse."* Our government officials do not have to tell you that you are being *"enslaved"* — or that you were *"volunteering"* to be a slave.

They simply asked you what status you believed you were in, in a very deceitful manner, utilizing a *legally presumptive leading question* — and you told them exactly what they wanted to hear:

"Yes, I am one of the serfs on the federal feudal Plantation!"

Tyranny exists when someone *tells you* that you are a slave.

They did not tell you that you were a slave; they asked *you* and *you* answered and *told them*!

Offense Classifications

In the United States there are <u>three basic classifications</u> of criminal offenses - <u>felonies</u>, <u>misdemeanors</u> and <u>infractions</u>. They are distinguished from each other by the seriousness of the offense and the amount of punishment for which someone convicted of the crime can receive.

Criminal offenses are further classified as <u>property crimes</u> or <u>personal crimes</u>. Elected officials on the federal, state and local level pass laws that establish which behavior constitutes a crime and what the punishment will be for someone who is found guilty of each crime.

What Is a <u>Felony</u>?

Felonies are the most serious classification of crimes, punishable by incarceration of more than a year in prison and in some cases life in prison without parole and even execution. Both property crimes and person crimes can be felonies. Murder, rape and kidnapping are felony crimes, but armed robbery and grand theft also can be felonies.

Not only can the person who committed the crime be charged with a felony, but so can anyone who aided or abetted the felon before or during the crime, and anyone who became accessories of the crime after it was committed, such as those who help the felon avoid capture.

Most states have different classifications of felonies with increasing penalties for the most serious crimes. Each class of felony crimes has its own minimum and maximum sentences. But anyone convicted of a felony also loses civil rights, including the right to bear arms and even in some states, the right to vote.

What Is a <u>Misdemeanor</u>?

Misdemeanors are crimes that do not rise to the severity of a felony. They are lesser crimes for which the maximum sentence is

12 months or less in jail. The distinction between misdemeanors and felonies lies within the seriousness of the crime. Aggravated assault (beating someone with a baseball bat, for example) is a felony, while simple battery (slapping someone in the face) is a misdemeanor.

But some crimes that are usually treated as misdemeanors in the courts, can rise to the level of a felony under certain circumstances. For example, in some states, possession of less than an ounce of marijuana is a misdemeanor, but possession of more than an ounce is considered possession with intent to distribute, which is a felony.

Likewise, an arrest for driving under the influence is usually a misdemeanor, but if anyone was hurt or killed or if it is not the driver's first DUI offense, the charge can become a felony.

What Is an <u>Infraction</u>?

Infractions are crimes for which jail time is usually not a possible sentence. Sometimes known as petty crimes, infractions are usually punishable by fines, which can be paid without even going to court.

Most infractions are local laws or ordinances <u>passed to deter dangerous or nuisance behavior</u>, such as setting speed limits in school zones, no parking zones, traffic laws or anti-noise ordinances. Infractions can also include operating a business without the proper license or improperly disposing of garbage or trash.

But under some circumstances, an infraction can rise to the level of a more serious crime. Running a stop sign might be a minor infraction, but not stopping for the sign and causing damage or injury is a more serious offense.

<u>Capital Crimes</u>

Capital crimes are those which are punishable by death. They are, of course, felonies. The difference between other classes of felonies and capital felonies is the fact that those accused of capital crimes can pay the ultimate penalty, the loss of their life.

Offenses

Uniformity in reporting under the Maine Uniform Crime Reporting System (MUCRS) is based on the proper classification of offenses reported to or known by the police.

The adoption of the National System of Uniform Crime Reporting included the utilization of the offense classifications of that system. Law enforcement in this state has made accurate application of those classifications in the reports submitted to the Maine Uniform Crime Reporting System.

In view of the need for compatibility with the National System, "offenses" under the program are now distinguished by designation of "misdemeanors," "felonies" or "municipal ordinance violations".

The explanations of offense classifications may vary slightly from language used by those familiar with Maine state law. However, the major categories of offense classification remain the same between the national and state levels.

PART I OFFENSES

Offense data consists of information that has been extracted from reports of Part I crimes that have come to the attention of Maine law enforcement agencies. In general, Part I crimes are usually reported to law enforcement agencies. Part I crimes are comprised of the following offenses.

1. HOMICIDE

1a.   Murder and Non-Negligent Manslaughter — The unlawful killing of a human being with malice aforethought.

General Rule — Any death due to a fight, quarrel, argument, assault or commission of a crime.

1b. <u>Manslaughter by Negligence</u> — The unlawful killing of a human being, by another, through gross negligence.

General Rule — The killing may result from the commission of an unlawful act or from a lawful act performed with gross negligence.

2. FORCIBLE RAPE

2a. <u>Rape by Force</u> — The carnal knowledge of a female forcibly and against her will.

General Rule — Forcible rape of a female — excluding carnal abuse (statutory rape) or other sex offenses.

2b. <u>Attempted Forcible Rape</u> — All assaults and attempts to rape.

3. ROBBERY

The felonious and forcible taking of the property of another, against his will, by violence or by putting him in fear. Includes all attempts.

3a. <u>Gun</u> — All robberies and attempted robberies involving the use of any type of firearm (revolvers, automatic pistols, shotguns, zip guns, rifles, pellet guns, etc.).

3b. <u>Knife or Cutting Instrument</u> — All robberies and attempted robberies involving the use of cutting or stabbing objects (knife, razor, hatchet, axe, scissors, glass, dagger, ice pick, etc.)

3c. <u>Other Dangerous Weapon</u> — All robberies or attempted robberies when any other object or thing is used as a weapon. (This includes clubs, bricks, jack handles, explosives, acid, etc.)

3d. <u>Strong Arm</u> — <u>Hands, Fists, Feet, Etc</u>. — All robberies, which include mugging, and similar offenses where no weapon is used, but strong-arm tactics are employed to deprive the victim of his property. This is limited to hands, arms, fists, feet, etc. As in armed robbery, includes all attempts.

4. ASSAULT

An assault is an attempt or offer, with unlawful force or violence, to do physical injury to another.

General Rule — All assaults will be classified in the following categories excluding assaults with intent to rob or rape.

4a.   **Gun** — All assaults and attempted assaults involving the use of any type of firearm (revolvers, automatic pistols, shotguns, zip guns).

4b.   <u>Knife or Cutting Instrument</u> — All assaults and attempted assaults involving the use of cutting or stabbing objects (knife, razor, hatchet, axe, scissors, glass, dagger, ice pick, etc.)

4c.   <u>Other Dangerous Weapon</u> — All assaults or attempted assaults when any other objects or thing is used as a weapon (clubs, bricks, jack handles, explosives, acid, poison, burning, and cases of attempted drowning, etc.).

4d.   <u>Hands, Fists, Feet, Etc.</u> — <u>Aggravated</u> — Assaults which are of an aggravated nature when hands, fists, feet, etc., are used. To be classified as aggravated assault, the attack must result in serious injury.

5. BURGLARY

Breaking and Entering — Unlawful entry or attempted forcible entry of any structure to commit a felony or larceny.

Note: For Uniform Crime Reporting purposes, the terms "Burglary" and "Breaking and Entering" are considered synonymous. All such offenses and attempts are scored as burglary. Do not score the larceny. Breaking and Entering of a motor vehicle is classified as a larceny for Uniform Crime Reporting purposes.

General Rule — Any unlawful entry or attempted forcible entry of any dwelling house, attached structure, public building, shop, office, factory, storehouse, apartment, house trailer (considered to be a permanent structure), warehouse, mill, barn, camp, other building, ship or railroad car.

5a.   Forcible Entry — All offenses where force of any kind is used to enter unlawfully a locked structure, with intent to steal or commit a felony. This includes entry by use of a master key, celluloid, or other device that leaves no outward mark but is used to open a lock. Concealment inside a building, followed by the breaking out of the structure, is also included.

5b.   Unlawful Entry — No Force — Any unlawful entry without any evidence of forcible entry.

5c.   Attempted Forcible Entry — When determined that forcible entry has been attempted.

6. LARCENY-THEFT (Except Auto Theft)

The unlawful taking of the property of another with intent to deprive him of ownership.

General Rule — All larcenies and thefts resulting from pocket-picking, purse snatching, shoplifting, larceny from auto, larceny of auto parts and accessories, theft of bicycles, larceny from buildings, and from coin-operated machines. Any theft that is not a robbery or the result of breaking and entering is included. Embezzlement, larceny by bailee, fraud or bad check cases are excluded.

7. MOTOR VEHICLE THEFT

The larceny or attempted larceny of a motor vehicle.

General Rule — This classification includes the theft or attempted theft of a motor vehicle, which, for Uniform Crime Reporting designation, is described as a self-propelled vehicle that runs on the surface of the land and not on rails. Excludes reported offenses where there is a lawful access to the vehicle, such as a family situation or unauthorized use by others with lawful access to the vehicle (chauffeur, employees, etc.). Includes "joy riding."

Excluded from this category are airplanes, boats, farm equipment and heavy construction vehicles, which are scored in the larceny category.

8. ARSON

Includes all arrests for violations of state laws and municipal ordinances relating to arson and attempted arson.

The willful or malicious burning to defraud, a dwelling house, church, college, jail, meeting house, public building, or any building, ship or vessel, motor vehicle or aircraft, contents of buildings, personal property of another, goods or chattels, crops, trees, fences, gates, lumber, woods, bogs, marshes, meadows, etc., should be scored as arson.

PART II OFFENSES

The Maine Uniform Crime Reporting System requires information on persons arrested and charged by municipal, county and state agencies on a monthly basis.

In compiling data for the monthly returns, the violations of municipal ordinances as well as state laws are to be included.

9. OTHER ASSAULTS

This class is comprised of all assaults and attempted assaults, which are simple or minor in nature. These "Other Assaults" are also scored on MEUCR-1 under item 4e as an offense known to police. However, for the purpose of this return, arrests for non-aggravated assaults are scored in this class.

10. FORGERIES AND COUNTERFEITING

Place in this class all offenses dealing with the making, altering, uttering or possessing, with intent to defraud, anything false in the semblance of that which is true.

Include:

- Altering or forging public or other records.
- Making, altering, forging or counterfeiting bills, notes, drafts, tickets, checks, credit cards, etc.
- Forging wills, deeds, bonds, seals, etc.
- Counterfeiting coins, plates, checks, etc.
- Possessing or uttering forged or counterfeited instruments.
- Signing the name of another or fictitious person with intent to defraud.
- All attempts to commit any of the above.

11. FRAUD

Fraudulent conversion and obtaining money or property by false pretense.

Include:

- Bad checks, except forgeries or counterfeiting.
- Leaving full-service gas station without paying attendant.
- Unauthorized withdrawal of money from an automatic teller machine.
- Failure to return rented VCRs or videotapes.

12. EMBEZZLEMENT

Misappropriation or misapplication of money or property entrusted to one's care, custody or control.

13. STOLEN PROPERTY: BUYING, RECEIVING, POSSESSING

Include in this class all offenses of buying, receiving, and possessing stolen property, as well as all attempts to commit any of these offenses.

14. VANDALISM

Vandalism consists of the willful or malicious destruction, injury, disfigurement or defacement of any public or private property, real or personal, without consent of the owner or person having custody or control by cutting, tearing, breaking, marking, painting, covering with filth, or any other such means as may be specified by local law. Count all arrests for the above, including attempts.

15. WEAPONS: CARRYING, POSSESSING

This class deals with violations of weapons laws such as:

- Manufacture, sale or possession of deadly weapons.
- Carrying deadly weapons.
- Furnishing deadly weapons to minors.
- Aliens possessing deadly weapons.
- All attempts to commit the above.

16. PROSTITUTION & COMM. VICE

Include in this class the sex offenses of a commercialized nature such as:

- Prostitution.
- Keeping a bawdy house, disorderly house or house of ill repute.
- Pandering, procuring, transporting or detaining women for immoral purposes.
- All attempts to commit the above.

17. SEX OFFENSES

(Except forcible rape, prostitution, and commercialized vice.) Include offenses against chastity, common decency, morals, and the like.

- Adultery and fornication.
- Buggery.
- Incest.

- Indecent exposure.
- Sodomy.
- Statutory rape — (no force).
- All attempts to commit any of the above.

18. DRUG ABUSE VIOLATIONS

Drug abuse violation arrests are requested on the basis of the narcotics used. Include all arrests for violations of state and local ordinances, specifically those relating to the unlawful possession, sale, use, growing, manufacturing and making of narcotic drugs. Make the following subdivisions of drug law arrests, keeping in mind to differentiate between sale/manufacturing and possession.

- Opium or cocaine and their derivatives: morphine, heroin, codeine.
- Marijuana.
- Synthetic narcotics, manufactured narcotics, which can cause true drug addiction: Demerol, methadone.
- Dangerous non-narcotic drugs: barbiturates, Benzedrine.

19. GAMBLING

All charges which relate to promoting, permitting or engaging in gambling. To provide a more refined collection of gambling arrests, the following breakdown should be furnished:

- Bookmaking (horse and sport books).
- Numbers and lottery.
- All other (include all attempts).

20. OFFENSES AGAINST FAMILY & CHILDREN

Include here all charges of non-support and neglect of family and children.

- Desertion, abandonment, or non-support.
- Neglect or abuse of children.
- Non-payment of alimony.

Note: Do not count victims of these charges who are merely taken into custody for their own protection.

21. DRIVING UNDER THE INFLUENCE

This class is limited to the driving or operating of any vehicle while drunk or under the influence of liquor or narcotic drugs.

22. LIQUOR LAWS

With the exception of "Drunkenness" (Class 23) and "OUI" (Class 21), liquor law violations, state or local, are placed in this class. Do not include federal violations.

Include:

• Manufacturing, sale, transportation, furnishing, possessing, etc.
• Maintaining unlawful drinking places.
• Operating a still.
• Furnishing liquor to a minor.
• Illegal transportation of liquor.
• Possession of liquor by a minor.
• All attempts to commit any of the above.

23. DRUNKENNESS

Include in this class all offenses of drunkenness or intoxication, with the exception of "OUI" (Class 21).

NOTE: Although "Drunkenness" and/or "Intoxication" offenses have been removed from a criminal offense category by the Maine Legislature, the category remains in the Uniform Crime Reporting Part II offenses and is to be used administratively. Persons taken into custody and/or referred to alcohol rehabilitation or "De-Tox" centers should be scored in this category by age, sex and race.

24. DISORDERLY CONDUCT

Count in this class all disorderly persons arrested except those counted in classes 1 through

25. VAGRANCY

Maine criminal code has eliminated this as a violation; therefore arrests should no longer be scored for this offense.

26. ALL OTHER OFFENSES

Include in this class every other state or local offense not included in classes 1 through 25.

- Admitting minors to improper places.
- Bigamy and polygamy.
- Blackmail and extortion.
- Bribery.
- Contempt of court.
- Discrimination, unfair competition.
- Kidnapping.
- Offenses contributing to juvenile delinquency (except as provided for in classes 1 through 25), such as employment of children in immoral vocations or practices, etc.
- Perjury and subornation of perjury.
- Possession, repair, manufacture, etc. of burglar's tools.
- Possession or sale of obscene literature, pictures, etc.
- Public nuisances.
- Riot and rout.
- Trespass.
- Unlawfully bringing contraband into prisons or hospitals.
- Unlawful use, possession, etc. of explosives.
- Violations of state regulatory laws and municipal ordinances.
- Service of warrants.
- All offenses not otherwise classified.
- All attempts to commit any of the above.

27. SUSPICION

Not reported in Maine.

28. CURFEW AND LOITERING LAWS

(Juveniles) Count all arrests made for violations of local curfew or loitering ordinances.

29. RUNAWAY (Juveniles)

For purposes of the UCR program, report in this category apprehensions for protective custody as defined by local statute. Arrest of runaways from one jurisdiction by another agency should be counted by the home jurisdiction. Do not include protective custody actions with respect to runaways taken for other jurisdictions.

CALCULATION OF RATES

The Uniform Crime Reporting program provides data for police executives to measure local problems. To facilitate this function, the local data must be converted into terms of rates and percentages. Simple formulas are presented which may assist in these computations.

CRIME RATES

One of the most meaningful crime statistics is the crime rate. This is the number of Part I offenses per 1,000 inhabitants. This rate can be calculated for any city, town or county.

To compute crime rates, divide the community population by 1,000 and divide the number of offenses in each class by that number. The answer is the number of offenses per 1,000 population and is the crime rate for that particular offense.

Example:

a.   Population = 75,000.
b.   Number of burglaries = 215.

Divide 75,000 ÷ 1,000 = 75.0.
Divide 215 ÷ 75.0 = 2.87.

The crime rate for burglary is 2.87 per 1,000 inhabitants. This same computation can be completed to give you arrest rates per 1,000 inhabitants.

CLEARANCE RATES

The percentage of crimes cleared is obtained by dividing the number of offenses cleared by the number of offenses known. This answer is then multiplied by 100.

Example:

a.   Number of clearances in robbery = 38.
b.   Number of total robberies = 72.

Divide 38 ÷ 72 = 0.528.
Multiply 0.528 ¥ 100 = 52.8.

The clearance rate for robbery is 52.8%.

CRIME TREND DATA

Local agencies can compute crime trends for a given offense for their individual agency for a particular period of time.

Example:

a.   Auto thefts in your jurisdiction for July through December last year were 21.
b.   Auto thefts in your jurisdiction for July through December this year were 29.

Subtract 29 – 21 = 8. Notice that 8 is an increase over the past year.

Divide $8 \div 21 = 0.38$. Always divide the difference by the total in the earlier time period.

Multiply $0.38 \text{¥} 100 = 38.0$.

Your trend in auto theft is a 38.0% increase for the last six months of this year as compared to the last six months of last year.

POLICE EMPLOYEE DATA

Police employee rates are expressed as the number of employees per 1,000 inhabitants of your city or town. To compute this rate, divide your population by 1,000 and divide the number of employees in your department by this number.

Example:

a.　Your jurisdiction's population = 75,000.

b.　Your agency's number of employees = 102.

Divide $75,000 \div 1,000 = 75$.
Divide $102 \div 75 = 1.36$.

Your employee rate is 1.36 employees per 1,000 inhabitants.

"The Grand Jury is both a Shield and a Sword."
— *Common knowledge of ages past.*

The Grand Jury as a Shield

True Justice requires "Acquitting the innocent & condemning the guilty." These are the words of the author of the Hebrew Torah found at Deut. 25:1. Just as equally important to condemning the guilty is protecting the innocent.

Furthermore, in Deut. 19, the judge must look out for a lying "malicious witness"; One who wants to "use the system" to jail and adversary. With this clause, and many other clauses in their Constitution (the Torah), the Hebrews *"Acquitted the innocent and condemned the guilty"* for approximately 800 years.

How important it is that grand jury members protect their fellow Americans from "overzealous" statutes and laws.

King Henry II started the grand jury system in England in 1166 to take indictment power out of the hands of the Catholic Church. This Act held only the "Shield power" and not the "Sword" — known as the *"Assize of Clarendon."* However, within a few years King Henry II started to abuse this system by issuing fines when his grand juries did not indict.

The founding fathers felt that the importance of indictment power should be taken our of the hands of the federal government so they places in the 5th Amendment the statement,

"No person shall be held to answer for a capital, or otherwise infamous crime, unless on a presentment or indictment of a grand jury..."

They did this so that the average person would be the protectorate of an overzealous government. The average person would be the person indicting a potential criminal.

The Grand Jury as a Sword

In a stunning 6 to 3 decision of the U.S. Supreme Court, Justice Antonin Scalia, writing for the majority, confirmed that:

The American Grand Jury is neither part of the judicial, executive nor legislative branches of government, but instead belongs to the people. It is in effect **a fourth branch of government** "governed" and "administered" directly by and on behalf of the American people, and its authority emanates from the "Bill of Rights" and has the power to enforce law and remove people from PUBLIC office.

> "If any of our civil servants commits a wrong against any one of the People in any respect, or breaks any one of the articles of security and peace, the victim of the transgression may ask any member of this grand jury to cause that error to be amended without delay. When the wrong has been shown to four administrators of this grand jury and those four administrators are not able to settle the dispute, those four administrators shall come to the grand jury and show the twenty-five members of the grand jury the error, which if sustained by the twenty-five, under the common law of the land, shall be submitted to the court to be enforced."
>
> — *From The Constitution of this Common Law Grand Jury*

MANUAL OF THE
COMMON LAW GRAND JURY
FOR CUMBERLAND COUNTY MAINE

LEX NATURALIS - DEI GRATIA

The constituted **CUMBERLAND COUNTY MAINE COMMON LAW GRAND JURY** (CC-CLGJ) is founded on the (41) precepts of the Grand Jury outlined by Justice Antonin Scalia speaking for the majority in the Supreme Court case, ***United States v. Williams*** *112 S.Ct. 1735, 504 U.S. 36, 118 L.Ed.2d 352 (1992).*

Justice Antonin Scalia

Precepts of The Grand Jury . . .

1) We the people [of the United States of America] have been provided with legal recourse to address the criminal conduct of persons entrusted to dispense justice.

2) The American grand jury is neither part of the judicial, executive nor legislative branches of government, but instead belongs to the people.

3) It is in effect a fourth branch of government "governed" and administered to directly by and on behalf of the American people, and its authority emanates from the Bill of Rights.

4) Thus, citizens have the unbridled right to empanel their own grand juries and present "True Bills" of indictment to a court, which is then required to commence a criminal proceeding.

5) Our Founding Fathers thereby created a "buffer" the people may rely upon for justice, when public officials, including judges, criminally violate the law.

6) Any power federal courts may have is very limited and does not permit reshaping the grand jury institution.

7) The "common law" of the Fifth Amendment demands the grand jury.

8) The grand jury is an institution separate from the courts, over whose functioning the courts do not preside; no such "supervisory" judicial authority exists.

9) Rooted in long centuries of Anglo-American history, the grand jury is mentioned in the Bill of Rights, but not in the body of the Constitution; it is a constitutional fixture in its own right.

10) The whole theory of the grand jury's function is that it belongs to no branch of the institutional government, and serves as a kind of *"buffer"* or *"referee"* between the Government and the people.

11) Although the grand jury normally operates in the courthouse and under judicial auspices, its institutional relationship with the judicial branch has traditionally been at arm's length.

12) Judges' direct involvement in the grand jury is generally confined to calling the grand jurors together and administering their oaths of office.

13) The grand jury's functional independence from the judicial branch is evident both in the scope of its power to *investigate criminal wrongdoing,* and in the manner in which that power is exercised.

14) The grand jury can investigate merely on *suspicion* that the law is being violated, or even because it wants *assurance* that it is not.

15) The grand jury need not identify the offender it suspects, or even the precise nature of the offense it is investigating.

16) The grand jury requires no authorization from its constituting court to initiate an investigation, nor does a prosecutor require leave of court to seek a grand jury indictment.

17) In its day-to-day functioning, the grand jury operates without the interference of a presiding judge, and deliberates in total secrecy.

18) The grand jury cannot compel the appearance of witnesses and the production of evidence, and must appeal to the court when such compulsion is required, and the court will refuse to lend its assistance when the compulsion the grand jury seeks would override rights accorded by the Constitution, or testimonial privileges recognized by the common law.

19) The grand jury remains free to pursue its investigations unhindered by external influence or supervision so long as it does not trench upon the legitimate rights of any witness called before it.

20) The Fifth Amendment's constitutional guarantee presupposes an investigative body acting independently of either prosecuting attorney or judge.

21) Certain constitutional protections afforded defendants in criminal proceedings have no application before this body.

22) The Double Jeopardy Clause of the Fifth Amendment does not bar a grand jury from returning an indictment when a prior grand jury has refused to do so.

23) The Sixth Amendment right to counsel does not attach when an individual is summoned to appear before a grand jury, even if he is the subject of the investigation.

24) Although the grand jury may not force a witness to answer questions in violation of the Fifth Amendment's constitutional guarantee against self-incrimination, an indictment obtained through the use of evidence previously obtained in violation of the privilege against self incrimination is nevertheless valid.

25) Over the years, we have received requests to exercise supervision over the grand jury's evidence-taking process, but we have refused them all.

26) We reject the proposal that the exclusionary rule be extended to grand jury proceedings, because of the potential injury to the historic role and functions of the grand jury.

27) We declined to enforce the hearsay rule in grand jury proceedings, since that would run counter to the whole history of the grand jury institution, in which laymen conduct their inquiries unfettered by technical rules.

28) Any power federal courts may have to fashion, on their own initiative, rules of grand jury procedure is a very limited one, not remotely comparable to the power they maintain over their own proceedings.

29) Any power federal courts may have does not permit judicial reshaping of the grand jury institution, or substantially altering the traditional relationships between the prosecutor, the constituting court, and the grand jury itself.

30) The grand jury's twin historical responsibilities are [1] bringing to trial those who may be justly accused and [2] shielding the innocent from unfounded accusation and prosecution that the Fifth Amendment demands.

31) Requiring the prosecutor to present ***exculpatory*** [*tending to establish innocence*] ***evidence*** as well as ***inculpatory*** [*incriminating*] ***evidence*** would alter the grand jury's historical role, transforming it from an ***accusatory*** to an ***adjudicatory*** body.

32) The grand jury sits not to determine innocence or guilt, but to assess whether there is adequate basis for bringing a criminal charge, and to make the assessment it has always been thought sufficient to hear only the prosecutor's side.

33) The grand jury is only to hear evidence on behalf of the prosecution, for the finding of an indictment is only in the nature of an *enquiry* or *accusation,* which is afterwards to be tried and determined.

34) It is not the grand jury's function to enquire or try the suspect's defenses, but only to examine upon *what foundation* the charge is made by the prosecutor.

35) The "common law" of the grand jury is not violated if the grand jury itself chooses to hear no more evidence than that which suffices to convince it that an indictment is proper.

36) Courts must require the modern prosecutor to alert the grand jury to the nature and extent of available ***exculpatory*** [*tending to establish innocence*] ***evidence*** because otherwise the grand jury merely functions as an arm of the prosecution.

37) The authority of the prosecutor to seek an indictment has long been understood to be ***coterminous*** [*coincidental*] with the authority of the grand jury to entertain the prosecutor's charges.

38) No authority exists for looking into and revising the judgement of the grand jury.

39) It would run counter to the whole history of the grand jury institution to permit an indictment to be challenged on the ground that there was incompetent or inadequate evidence before the grand jury.

40) The mere fact that evidence is unreliable is not sufficient grounds to require a dismissal of the indictment.

41) A challenge to the reliability or competence of the evidence presented to the grand jury will not be heard.

[End of Supreme Court quotes]

Other Precepts of Law

See Common Law Handbook for matching Citations.

1) No statue or rule prevents citizens from convening grand juries.

2) Presentment are filed with the Clerk of Court and once filed cannot be removed, and anyone interfering with an official proceeding commits a crime under US codes.

3) Trust in the jury is one of the cornerstones of our entire criminal jurisprudence even to the extent of jury nullification.

4) For there to be a crime, there must first be a victim (corpus delecti); in the absence of a victim there can be no crime; the state cannot be the injured party.

5) All power is inherent in the people; they may exercise it by themselves in all cases to which they think themselves competent; deciding by a jury of themselves, both fact and law, in all judiciary cases in which any fact is involved.

6) It is the "DUTY" of the Common Law Grand Jury to expose all fraud and corruption, whether it is in the political or judicial realm, and stop it!

7) The Authority of the Grand Jury is found in the Bill of Rights at Amendment V – "No person shall be held to answer for a capital, or otherwise infamous crime, unless on a *presentment* or *indictment* of a Grand Jury..."

8) The Grand Jury is the "ultimate power" of the people which allows them to *consent or not* to the actions of their servant government, by forcing the government to seek *permission from the people* before criminal charges can be filed; if the people refuse, it cannot go forward.

9) Governments are instituted among Men, deriving their just powers from the consent of the governed.

10) Every man is independent of all laws, except those pre-scribed by nature. He is not bound by any institutions formed by his fellowman without his consent.

11) There are only *three ways* a court can hear a criminal complaint:

> **1.** One or more of the people sign a sworn affidavit that they have been injured;
>
> **2.** A prosecutor, on behalf of the government, brings an accusation before the Grand Jury and the Grand Jury either indicts or does nothing;
>
> **3.** The Grand Jury, by its "own will", can investigate merely on suspicion that the law is being violated, or even because it wants *assurance* that it is not, and if it finds wrongdoing it can present it to the court *and it must go to trial.*

12) Any authority our servants have is by our consent; if they act outside their authority they are subject to criminal charges.

13) The Fifth Amendment states: "No person shall be held to answer for a capital, or otherwise infamous crime, unless on a pre-sentment or indictment of a Grand Jury."

14) Our US Constitution only authorizes "common law courts" a.k.a. "courts of record". A court of record removes the power of the Judge to make a ruling, his role is that of the "administrator" of the court. The final determinator is the "tribunal" who is either the "sovereign plaintiff" or a "jury".

15) The common law is the Supreme Law of the land, the codes, rules, regulations, policies and statutes are not "the law".

16) All codes, rules, and regulations are for government au-thorities only, not human/creators in accordance with God's laws.

17) All laws, rules and practices which are repugnant to the Constitution are null and void.

18) No one is bound to obey an unconstitutional law and no courts are bound to enforce it.

19) The term *"liberty"* denotes the right of the individual to contract, to engage in any of the common occupations of life, to acquire useful knowledge, this liberty may not be interfered with by legislative action, under the guise of protecting public interest.

20) A State cannot exclude a person from the practice of law.

21) The practice of law cannot be licensed by any state/State.

22) The practice of law is an occupation of common right.

23) The right to file a lawsuit pro se is one of the most important rights under the constitution and laws.

24) Litigants can be assisted by *unlicensed laymen* during judicial proceedings.

25) A *next friend* is a person who represents someone who is unable to tend to his or her own interest.

26) Members of groups who are competent *non-lawyers* can assist other members of the group achieve the goals of the group in court without being charged with *"unauthorized practice of law"*.

27) Every man is independent of all laws, except those prescribed by nature. He is not bound by any institutions formed by his fellowman *without his consent.*

28) The claim and exercise of a Constitutional Right cannot be converted into a crime.

29) The Sheriff is the Chief Law Enforcement Officer (CLEO) of the County.

30) The Sheriff is the Peoples' last line of defense against a government gone Rogue.

31) No action can be taken against a sovereign in the non-constitution courts of either the United States or the States; any such action is the crime of Barratry; Barratry is an offense at common law.

32) Whenever people are well-informed they can be trusted with their own government. — *Thomas Jefferson*

The United States exists in two forms

The United States exists in two forms: The *original united States* which controlled the federal government until 1860; and the *federal United States* which was incorporated in 1871.

The government of the *original united States of America* was usurped by the government of the *federal United States* which only controls the *District of Columbia and its territories* (Washington, D.C.) as a for-profit corporation that acts as our National Government. The *Corporate United States* operates under public *commercial law* rather than private *common law*.

The original Constitution and the Declaration of Independence refer to *"these united States"*. The word *"united"* is an adjective describing the noun, *"States"*. Therefore the lower case *"united"*.

When the *federal United States* was formed in 1871 the adjective *"united"* was changed to the noun *"United"* because the *federal United States* is a corporation which word is not an adjective but a noun.

The Constitution of the *original united States of America* was never removed; it has lain dormant since 1871 and is still intact to this day. This point was made clear by Supreme Court Justice Marshall Harlan in *Downes v. Bidwell* 182, U.S. 244 1901 by the following dissenting opinion: *"Two national governments exist; one to be maintained under the Constitution with all its restrictions; the other to be maintained by Congress outside and independently of that Instrument."*

The *rewritten* 1871 *Constitution of the United States (Inc.)* overrides the *original Constitution for the united States of America,* which explains why our Congressmen and Senators don't abide by it and the President (CEO) of the Corporate United States can write Executive Orders to do whatever he wants to do. He is following corporate laws that completely *strip* sovereigns of their God given unalienable rights.

Corporate public *commercial law* is not sovereign (private), for it is a public agreement between two or more parties under public contract.

Common law (under which sovereigns operate) is not *commercial law*; common law is personal and private.

Source: Black's Law Dictionary, Sixth Edition (With Pronunciations)

Government *De facto*. A government of fact exercising power and control in the place of true and lawful government; a government not established according to the constitution of the nation, not lawfully entitled to recognition or supremacy but which has nevertheless supplanted or displaced the government *de jure*. A government deemed unlawful or wrongful and unjust, which, nevertheless, receives habitual obedience from the bulk of the commune (community).

There are several degrees of what is called *"de facto government"*. Such a government in its *highest* degree assumes a character closely resembling that of a lawful government. This is when the usurping government expels the regular authorities from their customary seats and functions and establishes itself in their place and becomes the actual government of a country.

The distinguishing characteristic of such a government is that its adherents, who are warring against the government *de jure,* do not incur the penalties of treason; and under certain limitations the obligations assumed by them in behalf of the country, or otherwise, will generally be respected by the *de jure* government when restored. Such a government might more aptly be denominated a *"government of paramount force"* maintained by military power against the rightful authority of an established and lawful government; and obeyed in civil matters by private citizens.

They are usually administered by military authority, but they may also be administered by civil authority supported more or less by military force.

Source: *Thorington v. Smith,* 75 U.S. (8 Wall.) 1, 19 L.Ed. 361.

***De facto* Government** - A government that maintains itself by a display of force against the will of the legal government, and is successful at least temporarily in overturning the institutions of the rightful government by setting up its own government in lieu thereof, *Wortham v.Walker,* 133 Tex. 255, 128 S.W.2d. 1138, 1145.

Government *De jure.* A government of right; a true and lawful government; a government established according to the constitution of the nation or state and lawfully entitled to recognition and the administration of the nation although actually cut off from power or control. A government deemed lawful, rightful and just, which has been nevertheless supplanted or displaced, which receives not habitual obedience from the bulk of the community.

De jure - A condition in which there has been total compliance with all requirements of law; of right; legitimate; lawful; by right and just title. In this sense it is the contrary of *de facto*. It may also be contrasted with *degratia,* in which case it means *"as a matter of right",* as *degratia* means *"by grace or favor".* Again, it may be contrasted with *deaequitate;* here meaning *"by law",* as the latter means *"by equity".*

Source; IBID: Black's Law Dictionary, Sixth Edition (With Pronunciations)

How the Constitution was usurped by the Corporation

The CORPORATE UNITED STATES is not obligated nor accountable to the People except to make a profit for its stockholders as a corporation. The corporate interest does not benefit the people but uses the people and their labor to make a profit for the corporation. This corporation works in concert with the corporate courts and banks to usurp the people's wealth. The transfer of the constitutional authority of the money over to a private foreign bank (the non-federal Federal Reserve) has devastated our lives. This crime of taking the money authority away from the People must be corrected and authority restored to a constitutional form of government so our country can become prosperous once again.

From a speech in Congress in Congressional Record of March 17, 1993, Vol. 33, page H-1303, regarding The Bankruptcy of the United States, by Speaker, Representative James Trafficant Jr. (Ohio), addressing the House:

"It is an established fact that the United States Federal Government has been dissolved by the Emergency Banking Act, March 9, 1933, 48 Stat. 1, Public Law 89-719; declared by President Roosevelt, being bankrupt and insolvent.

"H.J.R. 192, 73rd Congress in session June 5, 1933 – Joint Resolution To Suspend The Gold Standard and Abrogate The Gold Clause dissolved the Sovereign Authority of the United States and the official capacities of all United States Governmental Offices, Officers, and Departments and is further evidence that the United States Federal Government exists today in name only.

"The receivers of the United States Bankruptcy are the International Bankers, via the United Nations, the World Bank and the International Monetary Fund. All United States Offices, Officials, and Departments are now operating within a *de facto status* in name only under Emergency War Powers. With the Constitutional Republican form of Government now dissolved, the receivers of the Bankruptcy have adopted a new form of government for the United States. This new form of government is known as a Democracy, being an established Socialist/Communist order under a new governor for America. This act was instituted and established by transferring and/or placing the Office of the Secretary of Treasury to that of the Governor of the International Monetary Fund. Public Law 94-564, page 8, Section H.R. 13955 reads in part: "The U.S. Secretary of Treasury receives no compensation for representing the United States.

"Prior to 1913, most Americans owned clear, allodial title to property, free and clear of any liens of mortgages until the Federal Reserve Act (1913) "Hypothecated" all property within the Federal United States to the Board of Governors of the Federal Reserve, in which the Trustees (stockholders) held legal title. The U.S. Citizen (tenant, franchisee) was registered as a "beneficiary" of the trust via his/her birth certificate. In 1933, the Federal United States hypothecated all of the present and future properties, assets, and labor of their "subjects," the 14th Amendment U.S. Citizen to the

<u>Federal Reserve System</u>. In return, the Federal Reserve System agreed to extend the federal United States Corporation all of the credit "money substitute" it needed.

"Like any debtor, the Federal United States government had to assign collateral and security to their creditors as a condition of the loan. Since the Federal United States didn't have any assets, <u>they assigned the private property of their "economic slaves," the U.S. Citizens, as collateral against the federal debt</u>. They also pledged the unincorporated federal territories, national parks, forests, birth certificates, and non-profit organizations as collateral against the federal debt. <u>All has already been transferred as payment to the international bankers</u>.

"Unwittingly, America has returned to its pre-American Revolution feudal roots whereby all land is held by a sovereign and the common people have no rights to hold allodial title to property. Once again, <u>We the People are tenants and share-croppers renting our own property from a Sovereign in the guise of the Federal Reserve Bank</u>. We the People have exchanged one master for another."

How can we repair our Country right now?

As the Republic for the United States works to re-install its government, the knowledge and truth about what has happened needs to be told. All Americans need to know the history of this tragedy, but with the good news about how it all can be brought back. Much help is needed to correct all of the unconstitutional laws, codes, and programs that plague our country today. The Republic for the United States of America is not a movement, it is the lawful government of the United States acting in the people's name. Become part of the re-establishment process; get involved with a Common Law Grand Jury and help to reactivate the Republic for the United States of America.

Soon to be Announced:

The National Economic Security And Reformation Act (NESARA)...

1. ...will restore Constitutional Law in the United States of America;

2. ...will require the current U.S. Administration at the national level to resign their positions to allow a fresh start; all Criminals in Government, the Cabinet and Appointees by the President, and all members of Congress are to resign within 72 hours of NESARA's Announcement;

3. ...will install Constitutionally acceptable President and Vice president Designates until new elections can take place within six months of NESARA's Announcement;

4. ...will abolish unconstitutional states of emergency;

5. ...will initiate the U.S. Treasury Bank System (TBS); with new U.S. Treasury Currency backed by precious metals;

6. ...will abolish the non-federal Federal Reserve; the Federal Reserve facilities and most Federal Reserve personnel will be absorbed into the Treasury Bank System of the United States;

7. ...will instigate the exchange of Federal Reserve Notes, which are not backed by gold, on a par for the U.S. Treasury Currency which is backed by gold;

8. ...will abolish Income Taxes in the United States and create a national sales tax on new, non-essential items as revenue for government; essential items such as food and medicine, and used items, are exempt from the sales tax.

APPENDIX

Nesara I
National Economic Security and Reformation Act

Authored by David E. Robinson

Long before NESARA, a project was born to restore the United States of America to its original Constitution of the Republic, and to remove the structure of the Corporate United States.

During the 1970's and 1980's many U.S. farmers were losing their land, machinery, buildings, and cattle due to fraudulent foreclosures by the Federal Reserve Banks, in cooperation with the IRS. Many farmers joined forces and brought a class action lawsuit against the U.S. Government, the non-federal Federal Reserve Bank, and the IRS, for fraud against the farmers.

Out of this restoration process came the Prosperity Programs, the Farmer Claims, and finally NESARA.

Order here: https://www.createspace.com/3676730

Nesara II
National Economic Security and Reformation Act

Authored by David E. Robinson

It is all coming down :

A cataclysmic shift in both Global Politics and Economics is now well under way. World Governments are coming to understand how the Global Banking System is systematically looting entire economies through theft, fraud, deception and manipulation, which in turn forces Governments to raise taxes that citizens should not have to pay.

Former Presidents and Prime Ministers of countries who have sided with the Banking Cabal, are now already jumping ship and supporting the growing movement toward proper financial management of the Global Accounts around the World.

Order here: https://www.createspace.com/3694967

Revocation of Election letter to the IRS

<YOUR LETTERHEAD>

<Date>   Certified Mail <0000 0000 0000 0000 0000>

Director of International Operations
Internal Revenue Service
Washington, D.C. (20225)

Subject: Notice of Revocation of Election and Request for Concurrence and Update to My Taxpayer Status.

Ref: 26 CFR 1.871-10

Dear Sir(s),

In accordance with 26 CFR § 1.871-10(d)(2)(iii), this letter is being submitted in pursuit of a Revocation of Election to treat any or all of my income and assets as a nonresident alien from being considered by the IRS as "effectively connected with a trade or business in the 'United States'", as defined in 26 U.S.C. §864(b).

Information about myself in fulfillment with the above CFR is as follows:

1. Name:
2. Address:
3. Former SSN:
4. Applicable taxable year(s):
5. Grounds for the request.

The Grounds for my request are My constitutional right to life, liberty, pursuit of happiness, privacy, respect, the fruits of my common right labors under common law, and the right to own and control property (including labor and the fruits of my labor) without any interference from government, or requirement to report, account for, such income or assets on such property.

This letter is by no means an admission in any way that I ever made an Election to treat any of my income or assets as effectively connected with a trade or business in the United States, but instead is submitted to ensure that my status is properly reflected in your records and that you do indeed concur with and respect this notification of request for your concurrence.

I do not now nor have I ever lived in the 'United States' as defined in 26

U.S.C. Sec. 7701, nor do I have any intentions of doing so in the future. I am sorry if I ever gave you the idea that I did by, for instance, mistakenly filing an IRS form 1040 in the past, which was the incorrect form. The correct form is and always has been the 1040NR form.

Please note that I already have an IRS form W-8 on file with my employer and have accurately declared myself to be a Nonresident Alien of the Corporation United States. I reside outside of the foreign jurisdiction to which the Internal Revenue Code (IRC) operates, which is the District of Columbia and federal territories.

"The United States government is a foreign corporation with respect to a state." (N.Y. re: Merriam, 36 N.E. 505, 141 N.Y. 479, Affirmed 16 S.Ct. 1973, 41 L.Ed. 287).

"In the United States of America, there are two (2) separated and distinct jurisdictions, such being the jurisdiction of the states within their own state boundaries, and the other being federal jurisdiction (United States), which is limited to the District of Columbia, the U.S. Territories, and federal enclaves within the states, under Article I, Section 8, Clause 17." (Bevans v. United States, 16 U.S. 336 (1818)).

"State: The term 'State' shall be construed to include the District of Columbia, where such construction is necessary to carry out provisions of this title." (26 U.S.C. Sec. 7701).

"United States: The term 'United States' when used in a geographical sense includes [is limited to] only the States [the District of Columbia and other federal territories within the borders of the states] and the District of Columbia." (26 U.S.C. Sec. 7701).

"A canon of construction which teaches that of Congress, unless a contrary intent appears, is meant to apply only within the territorial jurisdiction of the United States." (U.S. v. Spelar, 338 U.S. 217 at 222 (1949)).

"The term 'United States' may be used in any one of several senses. It may be merely the name of a sovereign occupying the position analogous to that of other sovereigns in the family of nations. It may designate the territory over which the sovereignty of the United States extends [324 U.S. 652, 672], or it may be the collective name of the states which are united by and under the Constitution." (Hooven & Allison Co. v. Evatt, 324 U.S. 652, 1945).

Foreign government: "The government of the United States of America, as distinguished from the government of the several states." (Black's Law Dictionary, 5th Edition).

Foreign Laws: "The laws of a foreign country or sister state." (Black's Law Dictionary, 6th Edition).

Foreign States: "Nations outside of the United States...Term may also refer to another state; i.e. a sister state. The term 'foreign nations', ...should be construed to mean all nations and states other than that in which the action is brought; and hence, one state of the Union is foreign to another, in that sense." (Black's Law Dictionary, 6th Edition).

Treasury Decision 3980, Vol. 29, January-December, 1927, pgs. 64 and 65 defines the words 'includes' and 'including' as: "(1) To comprise, comprehend, or embrace... (2) To enclose within; contain; confine...But granting that the word 'including' is a term of enlargement, it is clear that it only performs that office by introducing the specific elements constituting the enlargement. It thus, and thus only, enlarges the otherwise more limited, preceding general language...The word 'including' is obviously used in the sense of its synonyms, comprising; comprehending; embracing."

"Includes is a word of limitation. Where a general term in Statute is followed by the word, 'including' the primary import of the specific words following the quoted words is to indicate restriction rather than enlargement." (Powers ex re. Covon v. Charron R.I., 135 A. 2nd 829, 832 Definitions-Words and Phrases pages 156-156, Words and Phrases under 'limitations').

"In the interpretation of statutes levying taxes, it is the established rule not to extend their provisions by implication beyond the clear import of the language used, or to enlarge their operations so as to embrace matters not specifically pointed out. In case of doubt they are construed most strongly against the government and in favor of the citizen." (Gould v. Gould, 245 U.S. 151, at 153).

Almost a century ago, Congress declared that "The right of expatriation [including expatriation from the District of Columbia or "U.S. Inc", the corporation] is a natural and inherent right of all people, indispensable to the enjoyment of the rights of life, liberty, and the pursuit of happiness," and decreed that "any declaration, instruction, opinion, order, or decision of any officers of this government which denies, restricts, impairs, or questions the right of expatriation, is hereby declared inconsistent with the fundamental principles of this government." (15 Stat. 223-224 (1868), R.S. § 1999, 8 U.S.C. § 800 (1940). [1] Although designed to apply especially to the rights of immigrants to shed their foreign nationalities, that Act of Congress "is also broad enough to cover, and does cover, the corresponding natural and inherent right of American citizens to expatriate themselves." (Savorgnan v. United States, 1950, 338 U.S. 491, 498 note 11, 70 S. Ct. 292, 296, 94 L. Ed. 287. [2] The Supreme Court has held that the Citizenship Act of 1907 and the Nationality Act of 1940 "are to be read in the light of the declaration of policy favoring freedom of expatriation which stands unrepealed." Id., 338 U.S. at pages 498-499, 70 S. Ct. at page 296. That same light, I think, illuminates 22 U.S.C.A. § 211a and 8 U.S.C.A. § 1185. (Walter Briehl v. John Foster Dulles, 284 F2d 561, 583 (1957)).

Thank you for your prompt and expeditious processing of this Revocation of Election.

Please forward your certification and response to my address above. I respectfully request that you give a detailed explanation and legal justification of any determination or basis you might make regarding the disposition of this notification. This includes citing any authority you are exercising and the regulation or statute from which it derives, as well as any court cites, Treasury Decisions, etc that may be relevant to the foundation of your delegated authority for making a determination of disposition. This letter shall serve as formal legal notice that if you DO NOT respond within 45 days, then by your default and silence, the Revocation of Election is granted and there is no need to further contact us.

I affirm, under penalty of perjury, under the Common Law of America - from without the United States - that the foregoing is true and correct, to the best of my current information, knowledge, and belief, per 28 U.S.C. 1746(1); and,

I now affix my own signature to all of the above affirmations WITH EXPLICIT RESERVATION OF ALL MY RIGHTS AND WITHOUT PREJUDICE - UCC 1-308.

Respectfully,

Your name in Caps and Lower Case
FOR Your name in ALL CAPS.

Common Law Handbook
For Juror's, Sheriff's, Bailiff's, & Justice's

Authored by David E. Robinson

"ONLY THE PEOPLE" CAN SAVE AMERICA - WILL YOU?

THEN REGISTER WITH THE "NATIONAL REGISTRY" at:

http://www.NationalLibertyAlliance.org

We are establishing Common Law Grand Juries in all 3,141 counties in the United States of America. By doing this the people will move our Courts back to "Courts of Justice" and take 100% control of our government.

Watch the video "Power of the Grand Jury."

THE DUTY OF THE "COMMON LAW GRAND JURY is to right any wrong. If anyone's unalienable rights have been violated, or removed, without a legal sentence of their peers, the Grand Jury can restore them. In addition, if a dispute shall arise concerning this matter it shall be settled according to the judgment of the Grand Jurors, the Sureties of the peace.

Order here: https://www.createspace.com/4460643

Meet Your Strawman
And Whatever You Want To Know

Authored by David E. Robinson

If nobody has told that you have a Strawman, then this could be a very interesting experience for you.

Your Strawman was created when you were very young, far too young to know anything about it.

But then, it was meant to be a secret as it's purpose is to swindle you, and it has been used very effectively to do just that ever since it was created.

Order here: https://www.createspace.com/4466376

The UCC Connection
How To Free Yourself From Legal Tyranny

Authored by David E. Robinson

**THE 10 MAXIMS
OF COMMERCIAL LAW**

1. A workman is worthy of his hire.
2. All are equal under the law.
3. In commerce, truth is sovereign.
4. Truth is expressed in the form of an affidavit.
5. An unrebutted affidavit stands as truth in commerce.
6. An unrebutted affidavit becomes judgment in commerce.
7. A matter must be expressed to be resolved.
8. He who leaves the field of battle first loses by default.
9. Sacrifice is the measure of credibility.
10. A lien or claim can be satisfied only through (a) rebuttal by counter affidavit point by point; (b) resolution by a jury; or payment or performance of the claim.

Order here: https://www.createspace.com/4513142

Chief Justice Roberts On Obamacare and The IRS - Traitor or Patriot? - You decide.

Authored by David E. Robinson

Secret Presumption is the monumental problem Roberts has chosen to expose with his courageous ruling on Obamacare. And he did it now because our country is poised on the edge of a precipice - right now.

Compared to the absolute catastrophe of generalizing the secret taxing authority presumption, all the hell of Obamacare is merely one example, with an infinite number of the same kinds of tax laws right behind it, waiting only for Congress to vote.

Roberts also showed the SOLUTION to the problem, when he wrote that "The Framers created a Federal Government of limited powers, and assigned to this court the duty of enforcing those limits. But judgment is reserved to the people."

Order here: https://www.createspace.com/4569363

Handbook Of The Unified Maine Common Law Grand Jury: For The Maine Republic Free State

Authored by David E. Robinson

"If any of our civil servants commits a wrong against any one of the People in any respect, or breaks any one of the articles of security and peace, the victim of the transgression may ask any member of this grand jury to cause that error to be amended without delay.

When the wrong has been shown to four administrators of this grand jury and those four administrators are not able to settle the dispute, those four administrators shall come to the grand jury and show the twenty-five members of the grand jury the error, which if sustained by the twenty-five, under the common law of the land, shall be submitted to the court to be enforced."

- From The Constitution of this Common Law Grand Jury

Order here: https://www.createspace.com/4711090

Change Is On The Horizon
Dawn of the Golden Age

Authored by James Rink
Designed by David E. Robinson

This book presents James Rink's extraordinary three hour
Internet video **"Change is on the Horizon"** in book form.
You may want to watch the video before reading this book. Go
to http://tinyurl.com/9xld6u6 for the full version.

Part 1 - **Dawn of the Golden Age**
Part 2 - **The American Federal Empire**
Part 3 - **The Farmers Claim Program**

David E. Robinson
Book and Cover Design

Order here: https://www.createspace.com/4034178

Kevin Annett: The Birth of a New Era: The End of Papal Authority and Corporatism, and the Rise of a New Common Law Covenant

Rev. Kevin Annett
A Revolution is Launched in Maastricht, Holland

Issued through the Common Law News Service (CNS)

Maastricht and Rome:

Last Easter Sunday, in an action akin to Martin Luther's posting of his Ninety Five Theses, a lone figure placed a Proclamation on the door of the oldest catholic church outside of Italy, and **announced the end of an era and the birth of another.**

Like Luther, Kevin Annett is a renegade clergyman who is caught in a life and death struggle with the oldest corporation on our planet: the church of Rome. But unlike the defrocked monk, Annett represents a movement aiming to not reform that church, but abolish it entirely because of its "irredeemable criminal nature".

And that abolition was announced this past Sunday.

The manifesto posted by Kevin Annett on the door of St. Martin's catholic church is called the **Maastricht Proclamation**, and invokes both international law and the "law of heaven" to declare the legal and spiritual abolition of the Church of Rome. The Proclamation effectively nullifies the authority of the Roman Catholic church under the very laws and legitimacy by which the latter claims to operate. (see www.itccs.org, April 20, 2014)

But the repercussions of Reverend Annett's action go far beyond Rome.

Interviewed today in Spain, where he is meeting with eyewitnesses to Vatican crimes, Annett comments,

"The modern Vatican is really the creation of Italian Fascism, whose **Lateran Treaty in 1929 established the modern corporation called the roman catholic church: a de facto but legally fictitious and criminal body.** In turn, that criminal syndicate helped spawn the horrors of the modern corporatist era, starting with Nazi Germany and leading to the present global New World Order. So by legally and spiritually disestablishing the Church of Rome, we are also dismantling that corporatist Order and all of the de facto, tyrannical authorities in the world, whether they be corporations, governments, or private courts.

"In other words, the **Maastricht Proclamation** is really a call to arms to all people to re-establish lawful de jure society across our planet, under the supremacy of the divine law of equality and peace: what we know as the Common Law."

In effect, what began in Rome on a bleak February day in 1929 ended last Easter Sunday, when the terms by which the Vatican operates as an overt criminal syndicate were lawfully negated under the terms of International Law. So while the church may continue to function as a de facto power, it does so as a rogue criminal body with no authority, and no right to its own property, wealth or laws.

What does this new step mean for the twenty year campaign by Kevin Annett to expose and stop the murder and trafficking of children?

"It's a whole new ball game now" says Annett. "This isn't about trying to hold a dying system accountable anymore, but about creating a whole new world through a new Covenant.

"Once we put church and state on trial, we really declared war on the entire system. And like Napolean once said, whoever makes a revolution half way is just digging their own grave. So now we need not just our own peace officers to enforce our Common Law court verdicts; we need to mobilize humanity to take back our world and the law from the criminals who are destroying us and our children's future. **And to do that, we need to re-contract all our relationships.**

"So in truth, there are no more lawful authorities anymore, and we owe none of them allegiance. We need to remake such authority from the ground up, from among ourselves. That's why we call it the New Covenant. And that's what we've begun, with the Maastricht Procla-mation."

This new Covenanting movement has two fronts, one legal, the other spiritual. Annett calls these fronts the **"two arms of liberation"**.

"Humanity is sick and dying, from the inside out, because we have forgotten our innate sovereignty and our bond with creation and the Creator. Nobody can mediate or create that bond for another, and **justice is an empty shell without the personal capacity to be a just and virtuous man or woman**. Benjamin Franklin said that only a virtuous people could be self-governing, for with personal corruption always comes political tyranny. So the new Covenant recognizes itself as both a new law and a new spirit, one supporting and feeding the other."

In the wake of the **Maastricht Proclamation**, this re-covenanting movement of The Covenanters, is working actively to establish both common law courts and self-governing communities on the land that have declared their independence from existing authorities. As the seed of a new world, the Covenanters are working now in twenty one countries alongside the International Common Law Court of Justice and its Tribunal sponsor, the ITCCS.

As for Kevin Annett, he is clearly a happy man.

"It's been a long night, but it's always good to see the day break".

Easter Proclamation Abolishes Papacy
https://www.youtube.com/watch?v=1zvtuHT7Cl4

www.itccs.org
www.iclcj.com
www.covenantedcommunity.org

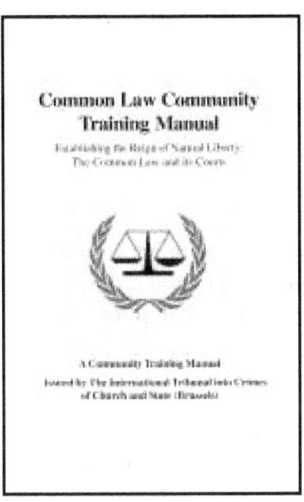

Common Law Community Training Manual

Establishing the Reign of Natural Liberty:
The Common Law and its Courts

A Community Training Manual
Issued by The International Tribunal into Crimes
of Church and State (Brussels)

Common Law Community Training Manual Establishing the Reign of Natural Liberty: The Common Law and its Courts

Authored by Rev. Kevin D. Annett
Prepared for publication by David E. Robinson

Many people are plagued by the injustice of the courts, police, schools, banks, social services and the NHS.

As citizens of a common law based judicial system, we have the right to come together in our local communities and convene a common law court in full lawful legitimacy.

We are capable of judging and sentencing any person, business or organization fairly regardless of the status they hold in society.

A court convened randomly by the public can be trusted to judge fairly with no alterior motives.

Order here: https://www.createspace.com/4707588

AFFIDAVIT

(sample for White Americans)

I, (name), being of sound mind and lawful age, do solemnly declare:

1. I am a freeman, born on the land of (State), of parents who were white, who were Citizen-Principals and whose parents time out of mind were and always had been white. As an hereditament I acquired directly the status of Citizen-Principal of said state sharing equally in its sovereignty. Slaughterhouse Cases, 83 U.S. 36 (1873).

2. As a white man, born on the land of (State), I am not restricted by the 14th Amendment, and because I receive no protection from it, I have no reciprocal obligation to a 14th Amendment allegiance or sovereignty and owe no obedience to anyone under the 14th Amendment. United States v. Wong Kim Ark, 169 U.S. 649 (1898).

3. I am a free Citizen of the aforesaid state of my birth and derivative and mediate thereof. I am also a Citizen of the united states of America as contemplated in the Constitutional Trust Contract of 1787.

4. I am not a citizen of the United States as contemplated by the 14th Amendment, and I do not reside in any state with the intention of receiving from the Federal government or any other party a protection against the legislative power of that state pursuant to the authority of the 14th Amendment.

5. I am, therefore, "nonresident" to the residency and "alien" to the citizenship of the 14th Amendment.

6. As the tax imposed in 26 U.S.C.1, pursuant to 26 C.F.R. 1.1-1, is on citizens and residents as contemplated by the 14th Amendment, it is not an applicable Internal Revenue Law to me, as I am neither such a citizen or resident.

Notwithstanding the fact that I may have in past years filed U.S. Individual Income Tax Returns, such filings were done under mistake by me not knowing that such filings were and are mandated only on citizens and residents of the United States as contemplated by the 14th Amendment.

7. Furthermore, I am not a resident of any state under the 14th Amendment and hereby publicly disavow any contract, form, agreement, application, certificate, license, permit or other document that I or any other person may have signed expressly or by acquiescence that would grant me any privileges and thereby ascribe to me rights and duties under a substantive system of law other than that of the Constitutional Trust Contract of 1787 for the united states of America and of the constitutions for the several states of the Union, exclusive of the 14th Amendment.

8. I reiterate that I have made the above determinations and this declaration under no duress, coercion, promise of reward or gain, or undue influence and of my own free will, with no mental reservation and with no intent to evade any legal duty under the laws of the United States or any of the several states.

9. I sincerely invite any person who has reason to know or believe that I am in error in my determinations and conclusions above to so inform me and to state the reason(s) they believe I am in error in writing at the location of my abode shown below

_ /
(Name) – sui juris, with express reservation of all my rights in law, equity and all other natures of law.

[Rights Reserved: UCC 1-308]

(address), (City), (State) [zip code] (County) (State of ?)

Signed before me this (?th) day of (month) 2013, by (Name), personally known to me and who did take an oath.

_ /
(Name of Notary

My commission expires (date) # (license number) Bonded thru (Insurance company)

NOTARY PUBLIC – STATE OF (?) — COMMISSION – EXPIRES

DECLARATION Of POLITICAL SOVEREIGNTY

(Sample for African-Americans)

I, (name), being of lawful age and of sound mind, do hereby declare:

I was born of parents of Black-African ancestry.

Prior to the ratification of the 14th Amendment to the U.S. Constitution, individuals of my heritage were held by the U.S. Supreme Court to be incapable of being or becoming Citizen-Sovereigns of the United States.

The 14th Amendment conferred upon individuals, such as me, the status of national citizen-subject and state citizen-resident.

I maintain that *Brown v. Board of Education*, 347 U.S. 483 (1954), in which the U.S. Supreme Court held that state laws that established separate public schools for black and white students were unconstitutional, by implication mandates that separate citizenship for white and black individuals is equally unconstitutional.

I, therefore, declare that I am a national Citizen-Sovereign and state Citizen-Inhabitant, equal in every respect to the same national and state status as white individuals.

I Declare the above to be true and correct under the penalties of perjury, 28 U.S.C. § 1746.

Done this __th Day of _____ 2014 at [city, state].

/s/_____

There is a legal maxim dating back to Rome, still standing today, that proves the truth of the points raised in my personal affidavit and in those that other Americans, of whatever background, race or heritage, may choose to file in their county records: *"silence deems consent.*

Maine Lawsuit Against The IRS
For Unfair Trade Practices

Authored by F. William Messier, David E. Robinson

COMMERCE consists of a mode of interacting and resolving disputes whereby all matters are executed under oath by sworn affidavit executed under the penalty of perjury as true, correct, and complete.

An affidavit is one's solemn expression of his truth. When you issue an affidavit you get the power of an affidavit. You also incur the liability involved.

An unrebutted affidavit becomes judgment in commerce. Proceedings consist of contests of commercial affidavits wherein the unrebutted points in the end stand as truth to which judgment of law applies.

Commercial Law is pre-judicial and non-judical.

A claim can be satisfied only through (1) rebuttal by affidavit point by point; (2) resolution by jury; or (3) payment or performance of the claim.

The conflict between Commercial Affidavits gives a clean basis for resolving disputes.

Order here: https://www.createspace.com/4014648

We the people by the mercy and grace of God ordained with certain unalienable rights, among them the right to form and exercise this 24 people Grand Jury in the spirit of the Magna Carta and our founding fathers and in obedience to God for this county on behalf of the people, having recorded our authority with the County Clerk and the State Supreme Court Chief Clerk by which we act in order to establish justice, insure domestic tranquility, secure the blessings of liberty to ourselves and our posterity by the securing of Natural Law and thereby returning Justice, Honor, and Grace for a perpetual administration of trust on behalf of the people hereby defined in this handbook.

<u>Rom 12:19-21</u> *"Dearly beloved, avenge not yourselves, but rather give place unto wrath: for it is written, Vengeance is mine; I will repay, saith the Lord. Therefore if thine enemy hunger, feed him; if he thirst, give him drink: for in so doing thou shalt heap coals of fire on his head. Be not overcome of evil, but overcome evil with good."*

Natural Law - *"Love the lord thy God with all thy heart, and with all thy soul, and with all thy mind. This is the first and great commandment. And the second is like unto it, Thou shalt love thy neighbor as thyself. On these two commandments hang all the law and the prophets."* - <u>Matt. 22:37-40</u>

Cumberland County Maine Grand Jury

Cumberland County Superior Court
Post Office Box 287
Portland, ME 04112-0287